GENERATION F*CKED

How Millennials and Gen Z Were Robbed of the American Dream and How We Can Fix Our Futures

FREDDIE SMITH

BenBella Books, Inc.
Dallas, TX

BENBELLA

BenBella Books, Inc.
8080 N. Central Expressway
Suite 1700
Dallas, TX 75206
benbellabooks.com
Send feedback to feedback@benbellabooks.com
BenBella is a federally registered trademark.

Printed in the United States of America
10 9 8 7 6 5 4 3 2 1

Library of Congress Control Number: 2026002028
ISBN 9781637748824 (trade paperback)
ISBN 9781637748831 (electronic)

Editing by Gregory Newton Brown and Claire Schulz
Copyediting by Scott Calamar
Proofreading by Ashley Casteel and Martha Gallant
Indexing by WordCo Indexing Services
Text design and composition by Aaron Edmiston
Cover illustration by Faceout Studio, Amanda Kreutzer
Printed by Lake Book Manufacturing

For my wife, Alyssa—my constant in a world that kept shifting. Thank you for your patience, belief, and love through every version of me.

CONTENTS

INTRODUCTION

The year 2020 changed the world forever. For me, it started in a dressing room at Burbank Studios just a few days before Valentine's Day. I was sitting with a black coffee in hand, sipping carefully from a lightweight Styrofoam cup so I wouldn't scorch my tongue. Rehearsal had just wrapped, and I was practicing my lines for the upcoming scenes that day, the familiar hum of production crackling over the intercom as they called the next actors to set. My turn was coming any minute.

A soft knock at the door pulled my eyes from the page. Standing there was one of our incredible production assistants, the same smiling face who'd handed me fresh scripts more than 750 times.

She passed me a brand-new script for the episode that we'd be filming later that week, and I sank into the couch, ready to see what was next for my character, Sonny Kiriakis, on *Days of Our Lives.* But as I read, a strange unease settled over me. With each line, my concern grew stronger.

Then I saw it. Sonny's final line: *"Goodbye, Salem . . . for now."*

Nearly a decade of employment gone in one sentence.

Those last two words—"for now"—gave me a sliver of hope that maybe one day I'd return. But the reality hit me fast: After having a steady paycheck on the show for nine years, I was about to be unemployed.

At home, I shared the news with my wife, Alyssa. After the initial shock, I tried to reframe it. "Things don't happen to you—they happen for you," I told her. Maybe this was my sign to start auditioning again.

I wrapped up my final week on set and said goodbye to the people I'd worked beside for years. It was sad and even a bit scary to move on, yet I also felt excited for the chance to see what other acting opportunities awaited me.

But life had other plans, because just one month later, the world shut down.

The headlines got darker by the day. Inside, I was doing my best to hold it together for Alyssa and my family, but it felt like the floor had collapsed beneath me. No job. No backup plan. And still hanging over me—a hundred thousand dollars in debt from a business manager who had drained my accounts four years earlier.

I remember thinking, *I had a higher net worth when I was nineteen than I do today.*

So we made a bold move: We packed up, left California, and started fresh in Florida in the middle of a global pandemic. But I quickly learned that rebuilding in the early 2020s was nothing like starting out in Hollywood in 2006. The bills were higher—rent, groceries, everything. Wages hadn't kept up. And for the first time, I truly felt the weight of the broken system we're all living in.

That's when it hit me: The middle class, the very dream my parents' generation built their lives on, it was gone. And if it was this hard for me, I knew it also had to be hard for millions of others. It was the summer of 2023, and I knew the American Dream as we knew it was dead.

But this book isn't an obituary—it's a battle plan.

Picture this: You're twenty-eight years old. You've done everything "right." You earned the degree, landed the "stable" job, and pinched pennies to save. Yet somehow, you're still drowning—buried under student debt that feels like a second mortgage, paying rent that eats half your paycheck, and juggling a side hustle that leaves you too exhausted to even think about retirement.

Then you scroll through Instagram, where influencers are taking luxury vacations and having these picture-perfect "adulting" wins, and you can't help but wonder: *Am I the only one who feels like I'm falling behind?*

You're not alone.

Millennials and Gen Zers are the most educated, tech-savvy, and socially conscious generations in history. But we're also the first to face a cruel paradox: working harder than ever while falling further behind. Wages have stagnated, but the cost of housing, healthcare, and education has skyrocketed. The old playbook—go to college, buy a home, retire comfortably—now feels out of reach for most people.

Meanwhile, we're often criticized for "killing" industries (goodbye, diamonds and golf), shamed for avocado-toast "splurges," and told to "hustle harder" in a system that has long forgotten about us. This isn't a whimper of victimhood. It's a rallying cry.

This book dives deep into why the American Dream died, who's to blame, and whether it was all a lie. Sure, uncovering these truths might feel depressing at first, but I'd rather you face these hard truths now, while there's still time to act, than wake up at sixty-five feeling behind.

One of the biggest challenges facing young people today is that the dollar doesn't stretch like it used to. Inflation has always been part of our economy. It isn't bad on its own—some of it is even necessary to keep the system running. But over the decades, it's quietly chipped away at what our money can buy and what stability really means for the average American.

Imagine this—your parents bury a time capsule in the backyard of your childhood home in the late 1960s. Inside are Polaroid photos, a baseball glove, a Beatles record, maybe a letter to the future. And tucked between those treasures? A crisp $100 bill. When you dig it up in 2025, the bill looks brand new, but here's the catch: $100 worth of groceries back then would now cost you more than $800. The bill is the same, but the value has quietly drained away.

That's the silent power of inflation. And yet, most of us were never taught this as teenagers.

We studied many important subjects in high school, but there was never a real focus on the one subject every student will need after graduation: money—how it actually works. How the financial system works, and how to invest and ultimately build wealth—a gap that still exists for most high schoolers today.

This isn't the fault of our wonderful high school teachers. They're crushing it. They're working with the curriculum they're given, teaching the lessons the education system has decided are top priorities. Those lessons are important for young adults to grow.

But leaving real-world economics out of the classroom is a massive disservice. The system has overlooked one of the most essential skills for thriving in today's economy: financial literacy.

I believe every high school in America should require a dedicated four-year curriculum in economics, investing, and money management—taught by a specialist, the same way we rely on math teachers for math, science teachers for science, and history teachers for history. In other words, we should have a money teacher for money. This isn't about changing what current teachers do; it's about recognizing financial literacy as a life skill and giving it the same seriousness and expertise as any other core academic subject.

Many schools already offer electives or partial coursework in personal finance, and those programs should absolutely continue. But in addition, we need a required course—*Money*—taught consistently and progressively across all four years of high school, with a standardized curriculum that ensures every student graduates understanding how money actually works.

And until that happens, the responsibility falls on us. Especially in a world where major corporations profit from our debt, it's more important than ever that we take ownership of learning these skills ourselves—and start passing them on to the next generation.

The truth is, most people want to save and invest for retirement—but with the cost of living so high, debt piling up, and wages lagging behind, it's hard to put enough away to make a real difference.

Here's the good news: There are ways to break free from this cycle. Later in this book, I'll share how you can fight back against inflation, grow wealth, and create a path to financial security—even in today's economy.

*!@X#

For me, it all started with a gut feeling back in high school. I remember sitting in class, staring at the clock, and thinking to myself, *There's no way I can spend the rest of my life doing something that feels this stagnant.* It wasn't that I didn't want to work hard—it was that I needed to move, to create, to feel alive in what I was doing. I knew I'd be better suited for something hands-on, something that pulled me out into the world instead of keeping me planted behind a desk all day. More than anything, I wanted a career that sparked excitement, so I started looking for another way forward.

In 2006, there weren't influencers, online coaches, or YouTube channels teaching you how to build a life outside the box. But in my senior year, a friend dragged me into a theater arts class, and something clicked. I'd found a passion that felt alive.

Three weeks after graduation, I packed my bags and moved to Los Angeles to chase an acting career. The next four years were a grind—survival jobs by day, five hundred auditions by night. Then it happened: I landed a role on *Days of Our Lives*. It was a dream come true. I was finally making money doing something I loved.

But there was a problem. Nobody had ever taught me how to manage that money. I didn't know the first thing about building wealth, and the financial mistakes I made during those years became some of the hardest and most valuable lessons of my life.

In 2014, my life unraveled. A near-fatal car accident shook me to my core, and worse, I discovered that my business manager had been stealing from me for years. She'd been sending me tax returns to sign, and every time money left my account, I assumed it was for taxes. It wasn't. She was pocketing the cash and never filing the returns. By the time I caught on, I owed the IRS three years of back taxes. In just twelve months, I went from feeling financially free to completely broke and $100,000 in debt.

I worked hard to dig my way out, but I still hadn't fully recovered when my run on *Days of Our Lives* came to an end just four weeks before COVID-19 shut down the world.

When my wife and I reached Florida, we were looking for a fresh start. She got her real estate license first, and I followed soon after, juggling sales with handyman work and DoorDash deliveries. But even making around $100,000 a year between us, we were still struggling to stay ahead.

It hit me one day, somewhere between showing homes and dropping off takeout: Back in 2006, working four days a week at Outback Steakhouse covered rent and a car payment, with money left for fun. By 2020, with two incomes, we were barely scraping by. Everything—rent, groceries, bills—was higher, while wages lagged far behind. For the first time, I truly felt the weight of the system and saw just how far the middle class had fallen.

As I struggled to start my professional life over, I found a front-row seat to the crushing weight Gen Z feels trying to start their lives at all. They're drowning in college debt; I was drowning in IRS debt. Their wages didn't come close to covering their expenses; neither did mine. But I thought I knew something they didn't—how it wasn't always this hard.

In 2023, I had a real estate client who was making $80,000 a year—a fantastic salary by most standards—who still couldn't qualify for a below-average home. I was stunned. So, I called the lender to see what was going on. Years ago, when my client first got prequalified, the home prices and interest rates were significantly lower, so the homes available in his price range were incredible. But now, he no longer qualified with that income. The lender walked me through the numbers: Record-high housing prices combined with rising interest rates meant you now needed far more income to qualify for a home than ever before.

That conversation lit a spark I'll never forget. I'll always be grateful to the lender that day—because the tools and insights he shared completely changed the trajectory of my life.

The very next morning, I sat down with a notebook and started running the numbers. I was fascinated by the puzzle of qualifying for a home loan—how income, down payment, interest rate, credit score, and even your debt-to-income ratio all fit together like pieces of a puzzle.

Then I found the number that stopped me cold: To qualify as a first-time homebuyer for the median US home, priced around $420,000 in the summer of 2023,[1] you'd need a household income of roughly $100,000, plus a $20,000 down payment—and that's assuming you have little to no other monthly debt (cars, student loans, credit cards . . . more on that all later). Yet the actual median household income in America was only about $80,000.[2]

It didn't add up.

I decided to break down the math in a TikTok video so I could help educate people who were trying to buy a home in this impossible market. Overnight, the video exploded—millions of views, thousands of comments, and a flood of interview requests from media outlets. The response was overwhelming. People weren't just interested, they were desperate for answers.

A week later, after a whirlwind of live TV interviews and features in major publications, I found myself at a family barbecue. Relatives patted me on the back, saying how exciting it was to see me on the news. In between bites of chips and salsa, I explained the heart of the problem: record-high home prices paired with 7 percent interest rates.

Today, the median household income simply can't qualify for the median-priced home unless they put down 20 to 30 percent and carry little to no debt. In practical terms, a $420,000 home would require a salary somewhere between $100,000 and $120,000 just to have a shot at qualifying. When you compare that to the reality of earning the median US household income—around $80,000—it's easy to see why so many buyers feel locked out of the market.

One family member—who bought their first home in the 1980s—nodded thoughtfully and shared with me that their generation faced challenges, too, like sky-high interest rates of 14 percent. "Buying a house has always been a challenge," they said.

They had a point. But later that night, curiosity got the better of me. I sat down determined to solve another puzzle.

I dug into the numbers from the 1970s through 2023, pulling historical data from the US Census Bureau, US Department of Housing and Urban Development, and Freddie Mac—and what I found shocked me. For the vast majority of those years, a median household income was generally enough to qualify for the median-priced home with a reasonable down payment. Even during the brutal interest-rate spikes of the early 1980s, affordability held together because home prices were lower relative to income and families carried far less monthly debt—no massive student loans, shorter car loans, and lower credit card balances.

But by 2023, that balance collapsed. The combination of record-high home prices, 7–8 percent interest rates, and today's heavier debt loads pushed many households far beyond traditional lending limits. For the first time in decades, the typical family was priced out of the typical home.

To put it in perspective: In 1980, the median home cost about $50,000.[3] A 20 percent down payment was just $10,000, while the median household income was around $18,000. Yes, interest rates were around 14 percent, which was brutal—but the savings hurdle was far more achievable. And by the early '90s, mortgage rates fell below 9 percent, allowing many homeowners to refinance and further lower their payments. Compare that to today: With a median household income of about $80,000 a year, a 20 percent down payment on a median-priced home of $420,000 comes to $84,000—an entirely different mountain to climb. Some buyers might choose to put down less than 20 percent, but that only raises their monthly payments—costs many can't afford or even qualify for. And while you can always search for a below-average home, in many parts of America, a $250,000 to $300,000 house simply doesn't exist.

And the challenge doesn't stop there. In 1980, the median single worker earned about $12,000 a year, and the median rent of $243 a month ate up around 24 percent of that income. Today, the median single worker earns about $59,000, but with rents nearing $1,900 a month, nearly 40 percent of their income could be gone before they can even think about saving for a down payment—stretching the path to homeownership further than ever before.

As we explore the failed economic policies that eroded the middle class, it's essential to extend an olive branch to the generations who came before us. If you're a Gen Xer or a boomer reading this, I want to thank you for being part of helping us find a solution. My goal is to help paint a clear picture of how small, seemingly minor policy decisions made over decades by our government and driven by corporate greed have snowballed into the financial crisis younger generations face today.

The truth is, we're simply living in a very different world than you did at our age. For the first time in modern American history, we are on track to be the first generation that, on the whole, will not surpass our parents' standard of living. That's not because we lack ambition or work ethic, it's because the economic ladder has been systematically pulled up, rung by rung.

Our generation quickly realized that something was broken, and it felt like it happened overnight. Just a few years ago, we were downloading TikTok and dancing to trends, watching season one of *Euphoria* and planning for our futures. But in the summer of 2023, the weight of the pandemic, surging inflation, and rising bills pushed many millennials and Gen Zers—including me—to social media to voice our frustrations about the economy. We didn't have to reach back to the '80s or '90s to remember "the good old days." For most of us, it was enough to think back to the early 2000s, when we were fresh out of high school. Rent could be found for $500, groceries for $250 a month, and it cost $20 to fill up a gas tank. Even during the 2008 crash, we scraped by on five-dollar footlongs from Subway and hope.

But 2023 felt different. This time, we weren't just tightening our belts, we were watching the cost of basic living explode. Social media feeds filled with stories of skyrocketing rent, grocery hauls where eight items cost $100, and endless examples of bills stretching paychecks to their breaking point. The momentum grew, and we realized we weren't imagining things; something was fundamentally broken.

As our voices grew louder, some members of the boomer generation took notice. Not all of them were impressed. Many had their own memories of economic struggle and, after decades of hard work, were quick to defend it. Phrases like "Just work harder," "Stop complaining," or "Cancel Netflix" became common responses. The back-and-forth sparked a generational tension that's still alive today.

The disconnect, I think, came from perspective. We weren't dismissing the effort and resilience it took for previous generations to build their lives, far from it. Our frustration was aimed at the *system* itself: decades of economic policies like "trickle-down economics" that simply didn't deliver, and the compounding costs of healthcare, education, housing, food, and utilities that have far outpaced wages.

So no, the boomer path wasn't easy—it was hard. But for many of us now, it's even harder. The only thing that's gotten cheaper over time are our "luxuries." Meanwhile, the essentials of life have become painfully expensive.

We are navigating a vastly different economic landscape than boomers did at our age. Since my wife and I once made a cross-country drive, let's use this road-trip metaphor for the journey through life. Boomers made that trip in a sturdy car—facing storms, detours, and breakdowns, but still moving forward with confidence. Their journey was tough, filled with hope, love, fear, and resilience, but ultimately, it led to stability.

And then there's us. We're traveling the same distance over the same terrain, but instead of a sturdy car, we're on a bicycle. Our challenges may look similar on paper, but they take us exponentially longer to overcome, and the energy required just to keep moving can be exhausting.

So what's the point in drawing this comparison? There are two reasons. First, I want to quiet the generational back-and-forth. Fighting each other isn't going to fix anything—it only distracts from the real problem: an economic system shaped over decades to funnel wealth upward, making the richest richer while squeezing the middle and working class. Second, the older generations currently hold much of the power required to enact change. They lead in government, run major corporations, and influence media narratives. Sharing our reality with them—backed by clear data—can help align our efforts toward a shared goal: a better future for everyone.

That's why our goal here is to reach the boomers who are still in positions of influence and help them understand that our reality is different from the one they came of age in. If some genuinely believe younger generations are just "lazy" or that the system works fine as it is, then how can we build the momentum needed to help the average American thrive again?

Think about it: Boomers still have their hands on the wheel in many ways. They make up a large share of political and economic power in America. In Congress, boomers account for about 39 percent of the House and nearly 60 percent of the Senate—despite representing roughly one-quarter of the population. They continue to lead the majority of Fortune 500 companies and shape much of our cultural and economic conversation.

And it's important to point out that boomers represent roughly seventy million people—a voting bloc with the power to shift the direction of the country. If we can bridge the gap in understanding, we have a real chance to work together to fix the policies and structures that are failing us all. Because when generations unite, the conversation changes—and so does what's possible.

This book won't just focus on housing. We'll dive into wage stagnation versus productivity, private equity practices, tax loopholes, media narratives, late-stage capitalism, the wealth gap, how we got here, and what we can do to fix it. I believe that the American Dream can be redefined and **rebuilt**—that work should open the door to stability, opportunity, and a better life shouldn't be a relic of the past. It should be a reality for every American, regardless of age.

Together, we have the power to make that happen. This is our chance to rewrite the rules, level the playing field, and build a future that works for all of us—not just the top 1 percent. It's about fighting smarter. Because if we're going to dismantle a broken system, we first need to understand the rules—then change them.

Chapter 1

SAME HOUSE, DIFFERENT REALITIES: THE NEW MATH OF THE MIDDLE CLASS

My wife, Alyssa, and I moved to Florida in October 2020, right in the middle of the pandemic. Like most people, we were trying to navigate our lives through uncertainty. At that time, housing prices, rent, and interest rates were still relatively reasonable. But, like many younger Americans, we weren't in a financial position to buy—we were carrying debt and focused on rebuilding our careers.

As the world began to reopen, there was a sense of hope. For a brief moment, it felt like we might recover quickly. But it wasn't long before the aftershocks of the pandemic reshaped everything. Prices surged, inflation skyrocketed, and the financial landscape shifted beneath our feet.

By the summer of 2022, I realized a truth that many of us are now struggling with: The middle class as we once knew it has changed forever. And it wasn't just the pandemic that caused this erosion—the pandemic was simply a magnifier, exposing a storm that had been brewing for more than fifty years.

Essentials—housing, childcare, healthcare, education—have steadily pulled away from wages. And while many of the consumer luxuries in the 1980s, like TVs and computers, have become cheaper over time (more on this soon), the necessities we actually depend on have only grown more expensive.

In today's post-pandemic economy, the pressure is even greater. Basic necessities like groceries, gas, and utilities are through the roof. Inflation numbers may be cooling, but the prices of eggs, milk, and gas remain stubbornly high. For previous generations—who had decades to build careers, savings, and investments—incremental price increases were manageable. For millennials and Gen Zers, even small upticks at the grocery store can blow apart a monthly budget.

We're not just contending with the old 2 to 3 percent cost-of-living increases. We're facing what I call **the Big Three:** housing, college debt, and daycare. These costs are at historic highs, far outpacing the inflation rates experienced by earlier generations.

1. **Housing:** Now eats nearly 35 percent of a typical worker's income, up from about 25 percent in 1980.[4]
2. **College debt:** Tuition and fees have skyrocketed since 1980, and outstanding student debt has ballooned to more than $1.7 trillion.[5]
3. **Daycare:** For families with two children, the cost of child care now exceeds median rent **in over thirty US states.**[6]

On top of that, everyday essentials have become dramatically more expensive since early 2020, before the pandemic hit: Grocery bills are up about 30 percent, rents are also up roughly 30 percent over the same period, and even gas prices—after falling from their 2022 highs—are still around 15 percent higher than in January 2020, which helps explain why a majority of Americans now live paycheck to paycheck.[7]

To see what this looks like in real life, let's take a drive through a classic all-American neighborhood tucked just off a busy main road. It winds into a picturesque community filled with cookie-cutter homes, neatly paved sidewalks, and the soft glow of streetlights at dusk. As you turn the corner, you notice three identical houses sitting side by side, each with a fresh welcome mat that looks like it came straight from Target.

At first glance, the homes are exactly the same—same layout, same square footage, same suburban dream. But inside? Their financial realities couldn't be more different.

Let's meet the neighbors.

HOUSE #1: THE BOOMERS (FRANK AND CINDY)

Frank and Cindy, a warm and easygoing boomer couple, bought their home in 1993 after Frank's company transferred him across the country. They snagged it for about $110,000—just under the median home price at the time. It was the classic early-'90s starter home: nothing fancy, but solid enough to build a life around.

Thirty years later, they've just celebrated Frank's retirement—right on schedule—and their mortgage is fully paid off. Their monthly housing cost now? Just property taxes and homeowner's insurance—about $700 a month. They go on morning walks, spoil their grandkids, and enjoy a level of financial stability that feels almost quaint by today's standards.

Same house. Same street. A completely different era of affordability.

HOUSE #2: THE GEN XERS (KEVIN AND MATT)

Next door, Kevin and Matt—a Gen-X couple—are in the front yard tossing a football with their teenage son, Chris. They bought the same model home back in 2015 for $250,000, using the $25,000 profit from selling their Chicago condo as their down payment.

Their timing was impeccable. In just a few short years, they refinanced during the record-low rates of 2021, their total housing costs—mortgage, taxes, and insurance—landed at $1,500 a month.

Kevin did go back to school later in life, so he's carrying a modest $300 monthly student loan payment. But with Chris in high school, they're long past the brutal daycare years. Their Big Three costs run $1,800 a month—about $21,600 a year. With Kevin's $90,000, they're doing more than fine. They save, invest, and take a couple of vacations a year. Their financial life feels steady and predictable.

Same house. Same block. A different set of tailwinds and timing.

HOUSE #3: THE MILLENNIALS (AMBER AND PHILLIP)

Now meet Amber and Phillip, the millennial couple unloading boxes from a U-Haul while their two little girls chase each other across the lawn. At thirty-six, they're thrilled to finally be homeowners—thanks largely to Amber's parents, who stepped in to help with the down payment.

However, their identical home—same layout, same square footage, same street—now costs $450,000.

Their mortgage, property taxes, and insurance come to $3,500 a month—more than double what their Gen-X neighbors pay. Add in $1,200 in student loan payments and $2,400 in daycare costs, and their Big Three expenses explode to $7,100 a month—or $85,200 a year.

Even with a combined household income of $140,000, once taxes, insurance premiums, and retirement contributions come out, there are months when they're barely breaking even. They use three budgeting apps just to make sure they can afford a couple of date nights a year.

Same house. Same street. But an entirely different economic reality.

Generational Expense Comparison

	Boomers (Frank & Cindy)	Gen X (Kevin & Matt)	Millennials (Amber & Phillip)
Housing cost	$700	$1,500	$3,500
Student loans	0	$300	$1,200
Daycare	0	0	$2,400
Total monthly Big Three expenses	$700	$1,800	$7,100

SAME HOUSE, DIFFERENT REALITIES

This is the generational wealth gap in action. Three identical homes, three very different financial realities—all shaped by nothing more than timing. This is where the American Dream quietly splits between generations.

Look at our three families. Frank and Cindy live a solidly middle-class life earning $48,000 a year because their big financial milestones happened at a time when costs were far more aligned with wages. Likewise, Kevin and Matt make just above today's median household income and are comfortably middle class not because they're wealthier or worked harder, but because their timing lined up too. Now compare them to Amber and Phillip. Even with a combined income of $140,000, their take-home pay after taxes, health insurance, and 401(k) contributions is roughly $8,000 a month, and the Big Three devour almost all of it.

All three families feel the pinch of rising grocery bills and gas prices. But for Frank and Cindy, it's a mild inconvenience. For Kevin and Matt, it's manageable. For Amber and Phillip, it's the difference between making the daycare payment or postponing another student loan bill. In fact, in this example, Amber and Phillip realistically *couldn't* afford to live on this street at all. They'd have to wait until their kids were out of daycare just to have a shot.

A $140,000 household income *should* put someone firmly in the upper-middle class. Instead, because of the Big Three, that income barely supports a middle-class lifestyle in much of the country. And when the median household income in America sits around $80,000, it becomes painfully clear why the middle class for people under forty is shrinking.

Millennials and Gen Z are renting into their thirties and older, delaying kids, postponing marriage, and pushing milestones further down the road—not because they want to, but because the math simply doesn't work.

So when younger generations say they need to make $120,000–$150,000 to feel stable, this is what they're talking about. And this is what they mean when they say it was easier for earlier generations—who built their lives during a time before decades of policy failures unraveled the foundation of the middle class.

WHAT "EASIER" LOOKED LIKE

When we say the economy was *easier* in the '70s, '80s, and '90s, here's exactly what we mean: Back then, homeownership wasn't a pipe dream—it was *expected*. Even during the high-interest-rate era of the mid-1980s, boomers were buying homes in their late twenties and early thirties.[8] Today, the median first-time homebuyer is thirty-eight—and in recent reports, that number is approaching forty.[9] At the age when millennials and Gen Zers are finally able to buy their first homes, boomers were already raising teenagers.

And if buying wasn't an option? Renting was *cheap*. Like, "spend

15–20 percent of your income on rent and still have enough left over to save for the future" cheap. Today, we're *lucky* if rent only eats up 30 percent of our income. Many of us are shelling out 40 to 50 percent just to live independently. And if that's not bad enough, *Business Insider* has literally dubbed millennials the "roommate generation."[10]

Sure, splitting rent with roommates when you're young and hustling makes sense. But when college graduates, business owners, and people fifteen years into their careers are still renting apartments because homeownership is out of reach? That's not a personal failure—that's a broken system.

And let's talk about the social implications. Back in the '80s and '90s, having people over was just part of life. Families hosted Thanksgiving dinner, friends packed into living rooms for football Sundays, and backyard birthday parties were the norm. Today? A 900-square-foot apartment with a balcony the size of a yoga mat doesn't exactly scream, *"Let's throw a party!"*

But it's not just about space—it's about stability. When you own a home, especially one that's affordable and comfortable, you escape the rent-increase rat race. No surprise hikes. No scrambling for a new place because your landlord sold the building to an investment firm.

For many of us, it's the opposite. We hold our breath every time we see a notice taped to the door, wondering if this upcoming lease renewal will increase our rent by another $200.

Back then, owning a home wasn't only part of the American Dream—it was a safety net. It was proof of progress. It was security. But today, millions of young Americans are stuck in a financial loop, paying sky-high rent with nothing to show for it. No equity. No wealth building. No long-term stability. Just financial anxiety on repeat.

And that's the part that doesn't get talked about enough: the hopelessness. The feeling that no matter how hard we work, we're just treading water. Many of us don't see a clear path forward, so we're basically winging it—crossing our fingers and hoping our 401(k) will be enough to retire by our late seventies.

That's not an economy that's *working*. That's an economy that's keeping us stuck.

THE GREAT LUXURIES SWAP

Our generation has earned a reputation for overspending. It's an easy conclusion to draw. Picture a twenty-seven-year-old filming a TikTok on their $1,000 iPhone, sipping a $7 latte, with a flat-screen TV glowing in the background as they casually mention just getting back from a three-day trip to Nashville. From the outside looking in, it's not hard to think, *Well, no wonder they're broke.*

That's when the common advice comes in: "Hey, maybe if you could ditch the lattes, budget better, and cut out the luxuries, you could get ahead."

Now, don't get me wrong—millennials and Gen Z aren't perfect. Some of us could absolutely benefit from better budgeting. If you're living paycheck to paycheck but ordering DoorDash three nights a week, that's overextending yourself. But for the most part, it's not the luxuries that are holding our generation back.

Here's the missing piece of the puzzle: Those "luxuries" aren't the reason most young people can't afford a home; they're simply the most visible part of our spending. The real problem runs much deeper, buried in skyrocketing fixed costs like housing, childcare, healthcare, and education—costs that no amount of skipping coffee runs can offset.

Forty years ago, life was cheap but luxuries were expensive. Now in 2025, luxuries are cheap, but life is expensive.

Back in 1985, Bob was paying $375 per month for rent, earning $2000 monthly. A "luxury" item like a brand-new high-end television set him back $700—equivalent to almost two months' rent.[11] Fast-forward to 2025, and the tables have turned. Mia pays $2,000 a month in rent on her $4,500 paycheck, but a television now costs just $200—a tenth of her rent.

Think about it. If Bob, back in the '80s, decided to deck out his home with three brand-new televisions for his living room, den, and bedroom ($2,100), a CD player ($400),[12] a microwave ($300),[13] a cell phone ($4,000),[14] and a personal computer ($2,500),[15] those "luxuries" would have set him back $9,300.

Now, to put that into perspective—that was equivalent to a 10 percent down payment on a $90,000 home at the time. If Bob's buddy came over and heard him complaining about not being able to afford a home, the advice would have been simple: "No shit, Bob. You just blew over two years' rent on gadgets!" Back then, spending recklessly on luxury items actually did impact your ability to buy a house.

But fast-forward to today.

Mia could go out and buy three flat-screen TVs ($600 total), a Bluetooth speaker ($30), a microwave ($200), a smartphone ($1,000), a laptop ($1,000), a new pair of shoes ($150), and a year of basic Netflix ($240) for $3,200. The difference? She'd still be more than $36,800 short for a 10 percent down payment on the median home today—not including the potential closing costs of thousands of dollars.

For Bob, luxuries cost two years of rent or a 10 percent down payment. For Mia, they cost less than two months' rent. The dynamic has flipped. The real luxuries now are rent, daycare, healthcare, and education—things we can't live without, and they're eating half our paychecks.

If we could trade cheap TVs for $800 rent again, most of us would do it in a heartbeat. But unfortunately, that's not the reality.

Many things today were considered extravagant luxuries in the 1980s. Technology, for example, was expensive.

A basic personal computer cost about $2,000 at the time, which is equivalent to more than $7,000 today. Now, you can get a far more powerful laptop for just a few hundred dollars. Home entertainment was also costly.

A VCR could cost anywhere from $500 to $1,000, which, adjusted for inflation, is like paying $1,500 to $3,000 today. Streaming services have now made unlimited content accessible for a fraction of that price.

Air travel was another luxury. A round-trip ticket from New York to Los Angeles could cost $600 or more, which would be the equivalent of more than $2,000 in today's money. Now, budget airlines offer that same trip for under $300.

Luxury cars were also far more exclusive. A BMW or Mercedes in the 1980s was a true status symbol, often costing the equivalent of $80,000 or more in today's dollars. Now, leasing a luxury car is common, and brands like Tesla have made high-end features much more accessible.

Compared to 2025, the main shift is that core essentials—housing, education, healthcare, and even food—have become much more expensive. Housing and rent, for instance, now outpace wage growth, making homeownership feel unattainable for many people. The cost of childcare has also skyrocketed, often equating to a second rent or mortgage payment for families. Food prices have increased as well, with staples like eggs, meat, and fresh produce costing far more than in previous decades. Insurance costs—whether for health, home, or auto coverage—have also risen dramatically. The fundamental issue is that wages have not kept pace with these increases, making it harder for people to afford the basics.

THE SHIFT EXPLAINED

This shift can be explained by a combination of technology, globalization, and "financialization." Advances in technology and automation have lowered the cost of producing high-end products like electronics, entertainment, and fashion. Globalization has allowed for cheaper manufacturing and outsourcing, which has helped reduce the cost of consumer goods but has had little impact on necessities like housing, healthcare, and education that remain tied to local economies. Perhaps the most significant factor is the financialization of necessities. Housing, education, and healthcare have been transformed into investment assets, driving up costs. Hedge funds now buy up single-family homes, universities operate like businesses, and the healthcare industry is largely dominated by insurance middlemen. As a result, luxuries have become more affordable, while necessities have become more expensive.

I do think older generations have a different perspective on luxury versus necessity as a result of these changes. They grew up in a time when hard work typically led to financial stability, whereas today, even with hard work, many people struggle with the high costs of housing, rent, and medical expenses. Because expensive things were rare when they were young, older generations often equate luxury with wealth. Today, it's possible to have an iPhone, nice clothes, or take a vacation while still struggling financially.

This is why millennials and Gen Z feel like they're constantly running on a treadmill—it's not necessarily about poor spending habits; it's that the economic game has changed. The inversion of luxury versus necessity is one of the biggest financial shifts in modern history. Older generations often view consumer goods as the ultimate status symbol, whereas younger generations see financial freedom as the true luxury. It's no longer about what you own but how much freedom you have.

WHAT WE'VE LOST

Once upon a time, companies actually took care of their workers. You put in thirty or forty years, and in return, your employer guaranteed you a pension—a monthly paycheck for life. It didn't matter what the stock market was doing. You didn't have to become an investment expert, rebalance portfolios, or worry about outliving your savings. You worked, retired, and collected your money.

Back in the 1980s, about 20 percent of jobs were unionized compared to just about 10 percent today. Union jobs weren't perfect, but they often came with real security: solid pay, job protections, and, most importantly, pensions.

I saw the power of pensions up close. My dad worked for Norfolk Southern, loading coal onto boats on Lake Erie. Thanks to his union, he had a steady paycheck, great benefits, and—unbelievably by today's standards—a pension. That pension is the cornerstone of my parents' retirement. They live in a small town in Ohio with their nearly $300,000 house paid off, and every month they receive guaranteed income. For example, if my dad were to receive a $5,000 monthly pension, my mom's benefit would be 50 percent of that amount—an additional $2,500 each month for life. That's not just surviving—it's comfortable living after decades of hard work.

Here's the magic of a pension: They don't have to stress over market swings, inflation, or whether their savings will run dry. The income is guaranteed, and it even has the potential to increase. If my dad passes before my mom, she will continue to receive his portion for the rest of her life. That is the kind of dignity and stability every retiree should have after putting in half a century of work.

Now, I know pensions aren't realistic for every job in today's economy. But after seeing firsthand the security they provide, I can't help but believe more unions—and more retirement plans that prioritize the worker—would make a massive difference.

The shift from pensions to 401(k)s was sold as a modernization of retirement planning, but in reality, it stripped away corporate responsibility and put the burden entirely on the worker. Corporations chose to keep their profits instead of keeping their promises.

Pensions vs. 401(k)s: The Bait and Switch

Pensions (What Once Was)

- Fully funded by the employer—workers didn't have to save a dime.
- Guaranteed lifetime income. No stock market stress.
- Encouraged loyalty and long-term employment.

401(k)s (What Most of Us Got)

- Funded primarily by workers. If you don't save, you don't retire.
- No guarantees—your future depends entirely on market performance.
- Employer contributions (if any) are optional and often minimal.

From the corporate perspective, this was genius. Companies could slash costs—no more fully funding retirement plans. They eliminate risk—if the market crashes, that's your problem, not theirs. And they could increase turnover—pensions kept workers loyal; without them, companies could lay people off more easily.

From the worker's perspective? It was a slow-motion disaster disguised as progress.

SO . . . WAS THIS A SNEAKY MOVE?

This shift wasn't some cartoonish, mustache-twirling villain-run scheme—it was marketed as "giving workers more control over their retirement." But let's be real: This shift overwhelmingly benefited corporations at the expense of workers.

The result?

Many boomers retired with guaranteed pensions. Millennials

and Gen Zers are far less likely to have that safety net, meaning the burden of retirement planning now falls almost entirely on the individual. Instead of relying on a steady pension check, younger workers are navigating a patchwork of 401(k)s, IRAs, and personal investments—all of which rise and fall with the market. And while these tools can build wealth, they demand financial literacy, discipline, and often higher incomes just to stay on track—advantages not everyone has.

Now, instead of steady pensions, we're told to hustle harder, invest smarter, and somehow save more—often while working in jobs that don't even offer retirement benefits. Meanwhile, many of the same corporations that walked away from pensions now pour billions into stock buybacks and executive bonuses. The safety net shifted upward, leaving workers to build their own.

At this point, you might be thinking: *Well, at least we still have Social Security*. And yes, Social Security remains the backbone of retirement for millions of Americans. But here's the reality—by 2033, the program is projected to cover only about 80 percent of promised benefits. That's because Social Security isn't backed by some giant trust fund locked away in a vault. It's mostly a pay-as-you-go system, where today's workers fund today's retirees through payroll taxes, with only a modest surplus fund acting as a temporary cushion. Once that surplus is depleted, the question becomes: Where will the missing 20 percent come from to keep promises to boomers, Gen X, and eventually us?

To keep full benefits flowing, the government will eventually have to either borrow more money or raise payroll taxes—both of which would hit younger generations the hardest.

It's tough to feel optimistic about retirement when the safety net we've been paying into for decades doesn't feel as sturdy as it once did. We'll dig deeper into Social Security later in this book, but for now, it's enough to say this: Pensions are disappearing, and younger generations are left carrying risks that once belonged to employers.

And that's where we turn next—because retirement security is just one piece of the puzzle. To really understand why life feels harder today, we need to look at how globalization reshaped the entire economy: lowering the price of luxuries while letting the essentials climb further out of reach.

A WORLD OF RISING COSTS: THE GLOBALIZATION GAMBLE

This brings us to globalization. These are the political decisions that shaped the world we live in today, and if we don't lay them all out, we're doomed to repeat history.

Globalization and offshoring chipped away at America's middle-class backbone. Factory closures and jobs going overseas hollowed out entire communities, especially across the Rust Belt. For many families, decades of stable employment disappeared almost overnight, and some never recovered. Even those who managed to hang on often watched neighbors lose everything.

The bigger issue with offshoring wasn't just that some jobs moved overseas—it permanently shifted the balance of power between companies and workers. Corporations could chase the cheapest labor around the globe, while American workers were left with fewer opportunities and less bargaining power. Yes, consumer goods like clothes and electronics got cheaper, but the trade-off was devastating: stable, middle-class jobs with good wages and benefits were replaced by lower-paying service work here at home. Cheaper TVs, but fewer people able to afford homes.

By the time millennials and Gen Z entered the workforce, offshoring had gone from rare to routine. The kinds of unionized, good-paying jobs with pensions that once anchored the middle class were already disappearing. Instead, we were left with service work, contract work, or chasing careers in industries just as vulnerable to outsourcing. Tech was supposed to be the "safe bet," but now even coding, IT, and legal work are sent overseas for a fraction of the cost. And on the horizon? AI—likely to disrupt our generation with the same force offshoring hit earlier ones.

Today stability looks more like a patchwork of 1099 jobs, side hustles, and self-managed retirement accounts. We have to learn tax law, juggle multiple income streams, and build our financial safety nets from scratch. And while that requires more education and discipline, it also means that if we plan correctly, we can create flexible financial lives that work on our own terms.

I learned this the hard way. My business manager once had me set up an S corp, and I had no clue what that even was. Payroll taxes, corporate filings, distributions vs. salary—it was overwhelming, and it made me vulnerable to being taken advantage of. Today, if you're new to gig work or self-employment, you can't afford not to learn these basics. This way we can thrive and set ourselves up for a comfortable retirement.

AND THEN THERE'S COLLEGE

We'll dig more into this later, but let's be clear: The math on higher education is broken.

It used to be common to work a part-time job and pay for school as you went. In 1980, a four-year degree at a public university cost about $4,000 total. Even at many private schools, the bill was closer to $10,000. Fast-forward to today, and the numbers are staggering: that same public degree now averages around $45,000, while private tuition can easily run $160,000 or more.

Plenty of grads walk across the stage owing $30,000 or more in student debt, only to graduate into a shaky job market. Some are delivering Uber Eats with their degree framed in the trunk. Others finish master's degrees but work retail because their industry dried up, their company downsized, or—my favorite—the so-called entry-level job requires five years of experience.

Starting salaries? Stagnant. The average college grad today starts at around $58,000 a year—barely enough to cover rent in most major cities. Tack on $200 to $300 in monthly loan payments that stretch over ten to twenty years, and it becomes clearer why people are delaying marriage, kids, and homeownership.

This is what happens when you stack bad policies, corporate greed, and decades of economic shifts on top of each other. The cost of everything that actually matters—housing, healthcare, education—has skyrocketed, while wages have barely moved. And unless we start having real conversations about it, nothing will change.

THE BIGGER PICTURE

Despite the economic challenges we all face today, I'm not hopeless. I'm simply asking the generations who came before us to hear our struggles—and to extend a helping hand—as we work to make the policy changes that will allow boomers to retire with dignity and give younger generations a real chance to thrive again.

We know boomers faced challenges of their own. They worked hard to pay the bills, raise families, and prepare for retirement. The difference is, they did so with a stronger safety net—affordable housing, union jobs with reliable benefits, pensions they could count on, and college tuition that didn't require decades of debt. If life was challenging even *with* those supports, imagine what it's like now—facing the same milestones with triple the obstacles and none of the protections.

If we can bridge the gap instead of shouting across it, we can work together to tackle the problems holding everyone back. We can push for housing policies that make homeownership attainable, reform student loans so they don't crush borrowers for decades, and ensure that raising a family doesn't mean financial ruin. That takes all of us—across generations—pushing in the same direction.

The American Dream isn't gone—it's buried under decades of economic choices that put profits over people. But here's the good news: The story isn't over. We can dig it up, dust it off, and rebuild it into something that works for everyone—today and for the generations yet to come.

And that's where we go next: into the heart of how the relentless pursuit of profit has shaped the system we live in—and how we can start rewriting the rules.

Chapter 2

AMERICA, INC.— PROFITS OVER PEOPLE

If America were a house, it would be the one on your block with the highest Zillow estimate. Fresh paint, new shutters, manicured lawn, expensive cars in the driveway. But step inside, and you see the truth: The foundation is cracked; the plumbing leaks; the roof is patched with duct tape. The market value looks incredible, but inside tells a different story.

We're told we're the wealthiest, most successful country in the world. And on paper, it looks true. GDP—the gross national product—is up. The stock market's booming. Corporate profits are at all-time highs. That's supposed to mean we're doing great.

But who exactly are "we"?

The truth is, America doesn't operate like a country—it runs like a Fortune 500 company. And like any massive corporation, it prioritizes one thing above all else: money.

A country is supposed to care about its people. A company cares about its shareholders. The United States picked a side.

That's why economic indicators can be glowing while everyday life feels harder. The system isn't designed to measure your health, your happiness, or your ability to raise a family. It's designed to measure how much value you produce for someone wealthier than you.

Jamie Dimon, CEO of JPMorgan Chase, in a 2024 interview told *The Wall Street Journal*, "The consumer's in pretty good shape right now. Unemployment's under 4% . . . Housing prices are up, stock prices are up, jobs are plentiful, wages are fine going up at the low end."[16]

For him and many other wealthy individuals, that's true.

But when CEOs, politicians, and pundits say the economy is strong, they're usually reading from the same script: GDP. Stock prices. Profits.

If those are your only metrics, sure—America's "crushing it."

Peel back the glossy veneer, though, and here's the reality:

- **More than two-thirds of Americans live paycheck to paycheck**—including some earning six figures.[17]
- **Savings are at record lows,**[18] while corporations report record-breaking profits every quarter.[19]
- **Housing affordability is collapsing.** Nearly 74 percent of Americans are dissatisfied with the availability of affordable housing,[20] and homeownership rates for young adults have plunged.[21]
- **Healthcare remains a financial minefield.** Medical bills are still the leading cause of bankruptcy.[22]
- **Fertility rates have fallen to historic lows,** largely due to the crushing costs of childcare and economic uncertainty.[23]
- **Education inequality persists.** College costs have skyrocketed,[24] and public school funding gaps leave millions behind.[25]
- **Teen mental health is in crisis.** According to the CDC's *Youth Risk Behavior Survey*, 39.7 percent of high school students experienced persistent sadness or hopelessness in the past year.[26]
- **The political divide is wider than ever,** turning fellow Americans into perceived enemies.

- **Trust in government has cratered**—only 16 percent of Americans trust it to "do the right thing" most of the time.[27]
- **Media incentives are broken**—outrage and division are more profitable than truth.

If we were truly the greatest country in the world, wouldn't these things matter more than quarterly GDP growth?

Instead of the "greatest country," maybe it's more accurate to call the United States what it really is: the greatest *corporation* in the world.

And like most corporations, it doesn't care if you can start a family, buy a home, or retire comfortably. It cares about the bottom line. Executives don't hold meetings to improve your work-life balance—they hold meetings to maximize returns. Even if that means layoffs, benefit cuts, or driving up prices for the very people keeping the system running.

The American economy works the same way. GDP growth doesn't mean life is getting better for most people. Corporate profits don't mean your paycheck is growing. Whether this "strong economy" actually benefits you comes down to two things:

1. Your age
2. Whether you own assets

Because in today's America, if you're young and don't own a home or stocks? It doesn't matter how "good" the economy is—you're still falling behind.

So when Mr. Dimon and others say "the consumer is in good shape," pay attention to the metrics they're using. In this chapter, we'll break down what those so-called success indicators *really* mean—and what they hide. We'll unpack:

- Why record GDP doesn't reflect everyday reality;
- How housing, healthcare, and education became unaffordable;

- What our collapsing mental health and trust in institutions are really signaling;
- And who actually benefits from this version of the economy.

Because a country built like a corporation might be great for the shareholders—but it's hell for everyone else.

THE STOCK MARKET: A GAME FOR THE FEW

Imagine this: You're at Thanksgiving dinner, and your mom's cousin leans back, swirls his bourbon, and says, "Man, I don't know why people are complaining. The economy is booming! My portfolio is up 40 percent this year!"

You glance at your bank account: Rent just cleared, your student loan payment is pending, and your savings balance sits at a cool $327. What economy is he talking about?

Beginning in November 2020, the S&P 500 climbed roughly 82 percent, hitting record highs by mid-2025. For anyone with a 401(k), IRA, or stock portfolio, that's been a huge boost. But here's the reality: About 93 percent of all stock wealth is held by the richest 10 percent of Americans—so while the market soars, most people aren't actually reaping the rewards.[28]

For the other 90 percent, stock market gains feel like watching a luxury yacht speed by while you're dog-paddling just to stay afloat. It's not that people don't want to invest—it's that the cost of living eats away at their paychecks before they even get the chance. When rent swallows 40 percent of your income, daycare costs rival a mortgage, and a single unexpected bill can derail your budget, investing becomes less about choice and more about survival. It doesn't mean people shouldn't try to prioritize it—you really need to—it just means the reality is far tougher than the sound bites suggest.

If you had an extra $200 at the end of the month, would you put it into an S&P 500 index fund—or pay off credit card debt racking up 24 percent interest? The stock market isn't a measure of how most Americans are doing; it's a scoreboard for the already wealthy.

Meanwhile, Main Street is stuck in neutral. Wages haven't kept pace with inflation, homeownership feels out of reach, and the price of everything—groceries, insurance, you name it—keeps climbing. But turn on the news, and you'll hear politicians and analysts brag about the "strong economy" because in their world, rising stocks mean everything.

This is the disconnect. Some see younger generations not investing and assume it's a choice. They don't realize that for many of us, investing feels like a luxury. And for those who do scrape something together to invest, they're starting late—missing those crucial early years of compounding—while carrying crushing debt and rising living costs.

So yes, investing is important—even under these circumstances, we have to find ways to build wealth wherever we can. But it's just as important to address why so many of us are struggling to do so in the first place. Because the more we pull back the curtain on the system, the more we see that the story we're told about a "strong economy" often leaves out the struggles most people face.

And nowhere is that clearer than in one of the government's favorite talking points: unemployment. On paper, the numbers look great. In reality? It's a different story.

THE UNEMPLOYMENT ILLUSION

As of mid-2025, the unemployment rate hovers just above 4 percent—a figure politicians love to tout as proof the economy is thriving. But ask most millennials or Gen Zers, and you'll hear a different story. We're employed, sure. But thriving? Hardly. Many of us are juggling two jobs or side hustles just to cover rent and groceries, let alone build an emergency fund.

Seventy-hour workweeks aren't about saving for a home or planning a vacation; they're about covering rent, affording groceries, and praying the car doesn't break down because there's no emergency fund to fall back on.

And here's the part that's dangerous: Humans are built to adapt. We adjust, we cope, we make it work. But there's a fine line between adapting and being taken advantage of. If we start accepting that working two jobs is "just how it is," then we've lost. That is not normal. That is not okay.

No one in America—especially not someone working full time—should be struggling to put food on the table or a roof over their head. But instead of fixing the broken systems that got us here, the conversation often shifts to blaming individuals. We're told we're lazy or don't want to work hard enough. But when have we ever said we want to work ten hours a week and live in a mansion with a Ferrari in the driveway?

"Well, wait a minute! Aren't you the generation fighting for a four-day workweek?" Yes—that is true, let's talk about why.

Since 1979, America's economy has become far more productive. Yet while inflation-adjusted productivity has climbed more than 87 percent, the typical worker's pay—including benefits—has increased by only about 33 percent.[29]

Computers replaced filing cabinets. Email replaced fax machines. AI now handles everything from customer service to legal contracts. Yet somehow, despite all these innovations, we're still chained to a forty-hour workweek—even when the actual workload could be done in less time. If technology is making businesses more efficient and profitable, shouldn't workers share in that progress through better working conditions, less stress, and more time with their families?

And here's the question that we should be asking: As AI and automation take over even more tasks in the next decade, are we really supposed to believe companies will finally give us shorter workweeks or better pay? History suggests otherwise—profits go up but expectations for workers rarely go down.

The push for a four-day workweek isn't just about technology. It's about the reality that so many of us already work two jobs just to survive. An extra day off isn't a luxury—it's a lifeline. Most people fighting for it aren't asking for less work; we're asking for a livable income from one job so we can actually see our families, enjoy our lives, and avoid burning out before forty.

Study after study shows a four-day workweek doesn't just benefit workers—it benefits companies too.[30] Employees are happier, healthier, and more productive. Businesses see higher efficiency in fewer hours.

We're not asking for handouts. We're asking for a system that reflects today's reality. We're asking for the same promise previous generations were given: work hard, buy a home, save for retirement, and enjoy the journey.

If a low 4 percent unemployment rate can't even get us close to that? Maybe the economy isn't as "strong" as they want us to believe.

THE HOUSING MARKET

I promise I'll move on from housing at some point—but it's just too important a part of the American Dream to skip over.

It's not only about ownership on paper (although in America, "ownership" comes with property taxes forever—so we never truly own it outright). It's about what owning a home *represents*. Ownership creates a sense of pride, stability, and connection. When people own homes, they tend to feel more invested in their neighborhoods and the nation as a whole.

I felt this shift firsthand when my wife and I bought in 2022 after being renters for seventeen years. I was a great tenant—paid on time, never caused issues—but I didn't think much about the community at large. That changed the moment we became homeowners. Suddenly, I was voting on where to put a "No Parking" sign on our street. When a Chick-fil-A and Starbucks opened nearby, we were genuinely excited—not just for the convenience, but because it signaled growth that could help our property values and our future. We've built stronger bonds with neighbors, too, because it feels like we're in this together, not just passing through for twelve months before the lease is up.

There's also the long-term hope of one day paying off the mortgage, lowering retirement expenses, and knowing we have a safety net in the form of equity. Even in a downturn, you can look at your home and think, *At least we're ahead.* With renting, it often feels like paying for a subscription you can't cancel—no matter how long you've been paying, you have nothing tangible to show for it.

Homeownership was supposed to be a cornerstone of the American Dream. But today, for many, it feels out of reach.

According to the Census Bureau, roughly 65 percent of households own their primary house—about eighty-four million households.[31]

Since the pandemic began, US home prices have surged over 50 percent, and the total value of the US housing market climbed from about $35 trillion in early 2020 to over $55 trillion by 2025—adding roughly $20 trillion in housing wealth for homeowners—one of the largest transfers of wealth in modern history.[32] Incredible news if you own. But for the one hundred million Americans who are renting, it feels like the ladder was pulled up even further.

For millennials and Gen Z, rising home prices aren't a win—they're a locked door. The "starter home" ladder keeps getting pulled further out of reach. Homes used to cost two to three times your annual income. Now, in many cities, they cost six to eight times as much.

Take Chris, thirty-five, married with a toddler and another baby on the way. For seven years, he and his wife have saved aggressively for a down payment. Back in 2017, they had their eyes on a modest three-bedroom for $275,000. They figured, give it a few more years, and they'd be ready. But by 2025, that same house is now priced at $450,000. Their savings didn't grow nearly as fast as prices did. Even after cutting vacations, dining out, and canceling their streaming subscriptions, they're still priced out and stuck renting.

Now, to be fair, as of 2025 there's a silver lining in some cities: Renting can actually be cheaper than owning—sometimes half the monthly cost of a mortgage once you factor in property taxes, insurance, and maintenance. But if you rent—whether by choice or necessity—you need to approach it with a *renter + investor* mindset. That means putting what you save on housing into investments, so you're still building wealth even without home equity. More on that later.

Still, for many renters, there's no "extra" money to invest. Millennials and Gen Zers often spend 30 to 50 percent of their income on rent,[33] leaving little room for savings. Back in my Outback Steakhouse days in Los Angeles, I could cover rent in a week of hard work. Today, in many places, it takes nearly two weeks of full-time pay just to cover housing.

The truth is the housing market isn't just expensive—it's structurally broken. Those who bought before 2021, or who had the means to enter the market earlier, have a huge advantage.

Consider Rosa. In 2010, she bought a modest house that needed a little work for $180,000 with a $45,000 salary,[34] using a 3 percent first-time homebuyer down payment—just $5,400. Eight years later, her home was worth $280,000. She sold it, pocketed $100,000 in equity, and bought her dream home—a four-bedroom with a pool—for $400,000. With the equity as a down payment, she financed $300,000 and later refinanced to a 2.5 percent rate, bringing her monthly principal and interest to around $1,200. In 2025, her home is worth $600,000. Even with higher property taxes and insurance, she's paying roughly $2,300 a month for a home worth far more.

That's the power of timing and leverage. Rosa built substantial wealth and stability off an initial $5,400 investment—simply by living in her home and letting the market work for her.

But that path is becoming rare. If the trend continues, homeownership could become something only the wealthy can afford. If housing is one of the most visible signs of the American Dream slipping away, GDP growth is one of the most misleading signs that everything is fine. Just like soaring home prices don't mean everyone's better off, a booming GDP doesn't guarantee that prosperity is reaching your bank account.

THE GDP MIRAGE: THE ILLUSION OF A THRIVING ECONOMY

Turn on the TV, and you'll hear politicians, corporate leaders, and the media brag about how "the country" is doing great. Most of the time, when they say, "the country," what they really mean is our *economic system*—capitalism—is doing great.

Try swapping their words in your head next time: "This new policy will be great for the country!" becomes "This new policy will be great for capitalism!" The meaning shifts.

Now, I understand the importance of capitalism and GDP growth. Done right, it can create jobs, spur innovation, and keep us competitive. But there's a fine line between fueling profits and neglecting people. Because what really is a country? It's not its profit margins—it's its people.

Both profits and people should thrive together. Yet, over and over, the talking heads focus only on the former. Politicians see us as voters. The media sees us as customers for advertisers. Corporations see us as workers. And when a downturn hits—or a private equity firm takes over—workers are often the first to go.

It doesn't have to be this way. We don't need to tear down the whole system. Plenty of it works brilliantly. But we do need to shift our intentions—from treating people as voters, consumers, and laborers to treating them as human beings who deserve better, especially in a nation with the world's largest GDP.

THE PROBLEM WITH GDP

If you want "proof" America is winning, look at GDP—gross domestic product. It measures all goods and services produced in a given time. Year after year, it grows, keeping the US at the top of the global wealth charts. Politicians wave it around like a gold medal.

And yet—how many of us actually *feel* wealthy?

If GDP is booming, why are wages flat, about two-thirds of Americans are living paycheck to paycheck, and millennials' median net worth barely cracking $50,000 while the top 1 percent gets richer?

Because GDP doesn't measure your well-being—it measures economic activity, no matter who benefits.

1. GDP MEASURES PRODUCTION, NOT QUALITY OF LIFE

It doesn't factor in wealth inequality, financial stress, or declining living standards. A country can have record GDP while its people drown in debt and can't afford homes. Sound familiar?

2. GDP RISES FOR THE WRONG REASONS

A hurricane wipes out a town? GDP goes up from rebuilding.

A medical crisis bankrupts thousands? GDP rises from hospital bills.

War breaks out? GDP surges from military spending.

Meanwhile, things that genuinely improve lives—family-leave policies, affordable healthcare, mental health services—barely move the GDP needle.

3. GDP GROWTH DOESN'T MEAN YOUR PAYCHECK GROWS

Since 1980, the US economy has more than doubled in size after adjusting for inflation. But wages for the typical worker have risen less than 20 percent in that same time.

4. COUNTRIES WITH LOWER GDP OFTEN LIVE BETTER

Sweden, Norway, and Denmark all rank higher in happiness, health, and work-life balance. Canada and Germany offer universal healthcare and affordable college. Australia has shorter workweeks and higher wages—all with GDPs smaller than ours.[35]

They focus on people, not just profits.

GDP: AMERICA'S FAVORITE DISTRACTION

GDP is the perfect political talking point—it makes everything *look* great while sidestepping the reality that most Americans aren't sharing in that prosperity. It's the same illusion as a company announcing "record earnings" while quietly laying off staff.

So here's the real question:

Would you rather live in the biggest economy on Earth or in a country where you can actually afford to live? In the wealthiest nation in history, we should have both.

TYING IT ALL TOGETHER: A BROKEN SYSTEM IN NEED OF A RESET

Step back and the pattern is clear:

- Stock market surges? Benefits the wealthiest 10 percent.
- Home prices skyrocket? Great if you own; crushing if you don't.
- GDP breaks records? Means little if wages stay frozen.

Millennials and Gen Zers aren't allergic to hard work—we've just been sold a dream that doesn't exist anymore. It's like trying to scale a thirty-foot wall with a six-foot ladder.

The fix starts with rejecting the idea that GDP equals prosperity for everyone. We push for higher wages, housing reform, and policies that protect workers, not just corporations.

If we don't, the American Dream won't just be fading—it'll be gone.

Because at the end of the day, GDP and corporate profits don't pay your rent—they don't fill your gas tank or cover your grocery bill. And that's where the real disconnect shows up: when even $20 an hour, once considered a solid wage, no longer stretches far enough to cover the basics.

Chapter 3

TWENTY DOLLARS ISN'T WHAT IT USED TO BE

In 2024, McDonald's in California raised its wages to twenty dol-lars an hour, sparking a nationwide debate. Back in 2006, when I was flipping burgers at an hourly wage of six bucks and change, twenty dollars an hour sounded like a fortune—because it was. At that time, twenty dollars an hour could comfortably cover rent and bills, and leave room for a social life.

When I moved to Los Angeles, one of my first jobs was working in retail at American Eagle for eight dollars an hour. That was tough in such an expensive state, but for a young actor chasing a dream, the holy grail was landing a serving job. Servers could pull in twenty dollars an hour or more with tips—and still have a flexible schedule. In 2009, I got hired at Outback Steakhouse. By 2010, I was serving tables, making twenty dollars an hour, and life felt easy. Rent was never late. I could grab dinner with friends three times a week, furnish my apartment, buy DVDs (yes, DVDs), take acting classes, and still save a little.

Today, that same twenty dollars an hour—adjusted for inflation—

would be close to thirty dollars. But here's the kicker: Even many people making thirty dollars an hour now are barely scraping by, and not just in expensive cities like Los Angeles.

Some folks—especially in the media—still talk about twenty dollars an hour like it's an incredible wage, and that workers should be grateful. For teenagers, entry-level workers, or people getting back on their feet, that rate can be solid. But for most Americans building careers, raising kids, and saving for the future, twenty to twenty-five dollars an hour doesn't cut it.

The disconnect comes when those with influence—politicians, CEOs, media personalities—haven't personally had to think about rent or groceries in decades. Just fifteen years ago, twenty dollars an hour *was* a strong wage, so it can seem "plenty" if you haven't run the math lately.

On a recent episode of the *PBD Podcast* hosted by Patrick Bet-David, Fox News host Jesse Watters asked, "So if a McDonald's worker is making twenty dollars an hour, is that six figures?" Maybe Jesse miscalculated on the spot. Or maybe it's the result of spending years surrounded by millionaires, far removed from the reality of everyday Americans. That's not to single him out—he's just one example of a larger problem: If the people shaping public opinion are out of touch with the numbers, how can we expect real change?

So let's break it down: Twenty dollars an hour working full time equals about $40,000 a year. After taxes, you're looking at about $2,700 a month. That might work for a twenty-year-old splitting rent with a roommate, covering basic expenses, and living lean. But for a family trying to pay for housing, childcare, and transportation, and save for a home or retirement? It's almost impossible.

And this is exactly why we have to look at wages with clear eyes. If the people in power think twenty dollars an hour is "elite," what does that say about the corporations setting those wages? And how do we push for progress when decision-makers are this far out of touch?

THE COST-OF-LIVING CRISIS

One of the biggest reasons wages feel stagnant isn't just inflation—it's the disproportionate rise in the cost of necessities, especially housing. When housing eats up such a huge portion of your income, it becomes nearly impossible to get ahead.

In 1980, the median rent in the US was about $243 a month including utilities.[36] The federal minimum wage was $3.10 an hour, meaning a full-time worker earned roughly $516 a month before taxes. Renting the median apartment would have consumed nearly half of their paycheck. That was steep, but with a roommate, the cost dropped to around 24 percent each—a manageable share. In fact, one week of work often covered an entire month's rent. That wasn't a luxury; it was the baseline everyone deserved.

But today, things are different. According to 2024 Census Bureau data, the median rent *including utilities* is about $1,487.[37] In many cities, especially for new renters, prices are higher—but to be fair and consistent, let's stick to the same data source. A full-time worker earning today's federal minimum wage brings home just $1,208 a month before taxes. That means rent alone would require 81 percent of their paycheck—literally impossible. Even with a roommate, two minimum-wage earners splitting $1,487 would spend 61 percent of their combined income on rent, which is still unworkable.

Now, to be fair, many states have raised their minimum wages. Take California, for example, where the state minimum wage is sixteen dollars an hour. That is progress—but it still doesn't go far enough when the median rent in California is roughly $2,600 a month.[38] Even if two minimum-wage workers shared that apartment, they'd be spending nearly 48 percent of their gross income on rent. Better than the federal case, yes, but still nowhere near comfortable. And it's a far cry from 1980, when two roommates earning the federal minimum wage could rent the median place in the US for about 24 percent of their combined income, utilities included.

Even college graduates—likely in a stronger financial position—aren't faring much better. The average starting pay for a new grad today, according to ZipRecruiter, is around twenty-four dollars an hour,[39] or about $4,000 a month. Paying $1,487 in rent eats up roughly 37 percent of their income. That's doable, but tight—hence why so many grads live with roommates.

Today, many young people spend four to six years in college, take on tens of thousands in student loans, and still end up needing a roommate just to afford the median rent. You'd think that investing time, money, and effort into earning a degree would at least guarantee enough stability to rent a one-bedroom without financial strain. But the cost of living has outpaced wages so dramatically that even those who go the extra mile aren't getting the basic stability that used to be accessible to workers of all wages in the past.

And that's really the heart of this conversation: Every worker, regardless of degree or background, deserves the same dignity previous generations enjoyed—the dignity of being able to afford a safe place to live without sacrificing a huge chunk of their paycheck. What people are fighting for isn't some new, radical idea. It's the simple, proven reality that worked for decades in this country.

Affordable rent isn't just about comfort—it's about giving people a chance to build savings, start families, plan for the future, and move through life with momentum instead of feeling stuck in place. That's what the American Dream was supposed to guarantee, and it's what millions are struggling to reclaim today.

THE REALITY OF MIDDLE-CLASS BUDGETS

Jeff and Simon, both thirty-four and college educated, live in Cleveland, Ohio. Their household income is $150,000 per year—solidly above the median. But after taxes, health insurance, and 401(k) contributions, their take-home pay shrinks to $95,000 annually, or about $7,920 per month.

Their Monthly Expenses:

- Rent and utilities (two-bedroom apartment): $2,500
- Student loan payments ($90,000 total): $925
- Daycare (two children): $2,400
- Groceries (family of four): $1,200
- Car payment (one car): $450
- Car insurance (two cars): $350
- Cell phones: $200
- Gas: $250
- **Total: $8,275 per month**

Even with a household income of $150,000, Jeff and Simon are running a $350 deficit every month. And that's before accounting for unexpected costs like medical bills, car repairs, or a weekend trip. Plus, Jeff and Simon have no credit card debt and one car paid off!

THE SINGLE-EARNER STRUGGLE

Contrast that with Mae, a single twenty-six-year-old who skipped college and went straight into the workforce. She earns $45,000 a year—the average salary for her generation. After taxes, health insurance, and 401(k) contributions, she takes home $2,649 a month.

Her Monthly Expenses:

- Rent and utilities (her half of a two-bedroom apartment): $1,200
- Groceries: $400
- Car payment: $350
- Car insurance: $175
- Cell phone: $80
- Gas: $150

- Credit card payments: **$350**
- **Total: $2,705 per month**

Mae is $56 in the red every month—before factoring in things like clothing, savings, or surprise expenses. Her reality mirrors that of millions of young Americans: barely scraping by, no matter how hard they work.

The point I keep hammering home is this: We cannot allow society, the government, and corporations to gaslight us into believing that working two jobs just to survive is normal. We've stayed quiet for decades, and look where it's led us—stagnant wages, skyrocketing costs, and an entire generation fighting just to stay afloat.

And we have to think about the message this sends to younger Gen Z and Gen Alpha. They're watching their siblings and parents do everything "right"—go to school, work hard, take risks, and in many cases invest tens of thousands into college—only to end up stressed, overworked, and barely getting ahead.

For decades, one of the big motivators to work hard was the lifestyle that came with success. The gold at the end of the rainbow was real: a nice house, a fancy car, dinners out every weekend, good clothes, long vacations, maybe even a second home with a jet ski at the dock. That vision motivated people to push themselves, take risks, and step out of their comfort zone to reach that $100,000 milestone.

But today? Earning $100,000—or even $150,000—in many states offers the same lifestyle that an average middle-class American enjoyed just twenty years ago on a much smaller salary. Back in 2015, $50,000 a year, with reasonable budgeting, could buy a home and even allow one spouse to stay home with the kids. That "$50,000 life" now costs closer to $100,000–$150,000. And if you want the old-school upper-middle-class lifestyle, you're now looking at an income of $200,000–$300,000—a level of earnings that's rare today. Not long ago, $50,000 was common, and $100,000 was comfortably within reach for many.

If this downward trajectory continues, what will the "new normal" look like for our kids? Will they be expected to work sixty, seventy, even eighty hours a week just to afford a basic life?

And here's the part no one talks about—we're standing on the edge of a massive technological revolution. AI and automation are set to radically increase productivity. On paper, that should be great news: more efficiency, more profits, more opportunity. But history tells us a different story. If past trends hold, corporations will pocket the gains while wages stay frozen.

So the question isn't just what's happening now—it's what happens next.

THE PRODUCTIVITY PAY GAP: WHERE DID THE MONEY GO?

Let's zoom in on the biggest heist of the last fifty years—one that didn't involve hackers, bank vaults, or ski masks.

As mentioned previously, since 1979, worker productivity in the US has skyrocketed by 87 percent—driven by technology, automation, and the internet. In theory, that should have meant bigger paychecks, shorter workweeks, and a better quality of life. But it didn't. Adjusted for inflation, pay for the typical worker—including benefits—has risen only about 33 percent.[40]

The reality is that the same workers, putting in the same hours, are producing vastly more—but capturing only a fraction of the gains.

This shift really started in the late 1970s and carried to today. Before that, from the 1940s through the 1970s, wages and productivity grew side by side. Between 1948 and 1979, productivity rose about 108 percent, while worker compensation rose about 93 percent—nearly the same pace. That's why so many young people today are frustrated and fighting for higher wages: We're producing more than ever, yet our paychecks haven't kept up.

So what does that gap actually look like in real life? Here's a way to picture the productivity-versus-pay story in simple terms. Imagine Company XYZ mirrors the modern American economy.

Let's say this small business has two employees making $50,000 each. Together, they bring in $1 million a year in revenue. Then the company adopts a powerful new tool. Suddenly, those same two workers—still putting in the same forty-hour weeks—become 87 percent more productive. The company's revenue jumps to $1.87 million.

But their pay rises only about 33 percent, from $50,000 to $66,500 each. Together, the workers created an extra $870,000 in value—but they only kept $33,000 of it. The rest flowed somewhere else.

That's the American story. For decades, every generation has embraced technology and innovation, helping this country and its companies grow richer. But for most workers, the reward has been crumbs—a little more pay for a lot more productivity.

And for the lowest-paid workers, it's even worse. If the federal minimum wage had kept pace with economy-wide productivity since 1968—the last time it tracked worker output—it would be over $23 an hour, not a measly $7.25.

And when the floor rises, everything above it rises too. If pay across the workforce had kept up in the same way, the average American worker wouldn't be scraping by on around $50,000 a year—they'd be earning something much closer to $100,000.

But where did all that extra wealth go? A big portion went straight into corporate profits, stock buybacks, and executive bonuses—rewarding investors and executives far more than the workers who helped create it.

Let's take a walk down memory lane. Meet Dan, a factory worker in the 1970s. Dan put in his forty hours a week at the local steel plant and, for his hard work, he earned enough to buy a modest three-bedroom home, take his wife and kids on a summer road trip, and still stash money into savings. His company even offered a pension.

Now, fast-forward to 2025. That same steel plant is long gone, outsourced to another country to maximize shareholder profits. The new "Dan" is Jason, a warehouse worker for a massive corporation. He works just as hard, but now he's making eighteen dollars an hour, struggling to afford rent on a one-bedroom apartment, and picking up Uber shifts just to cover his student loan payments. His company? It just announced record profits for the tenth quarter in a row. The CEO? He took home a $20 million bonus—on top of his $30 million salary.

And it's not just Jason. Across every industry, workers are pulling double the weight for a fraction of the reward. In the 1960s, the average CEO made about twenty times what their workers did. Today? The average CEO makes *399 times* what their employees make.[41] And while executive salaries have skyrocketed, real wages for the working class have barely moved.

Yes, I understand and agree that CEOs and business owners who took the risks to start a company should make more money. They built something, and they deserve to be compensated for that. But here's the question: Why isn't a salary of fifty times the average worker enough? I mean, that's still $2.5 million a year! How did we get to a place where the average CEO now makes nearly 400 times what their employees do? Crazy! It should be common sense—and common decency—that if workers help build a corporation's empire, they should be rewarded accordingly. Yet, quarter after quarter, corporations boast record-breaking profits, stock buybacks, and executive bonuses, while the people who actually keep the company running see wages that barely keep up with inflation. And let's not forget—the little money we do get is taxed a million and one ways.

Even if we put aside the fact that these companies are greedy and exploiting their workforce, there's another glaring issue: The average worker gets a 2–3 percent raise per year, which barely covers inflation. If inflation rises by 2–3 percent and your pay increases by 3 percent, your spending power stays exactly the same. You're running in place. But executives? Shareholders? They're seeing double-digit increases in their earnings and stock dividends—far outpacing inflation.

Let's take a recent example of inflation. Between January 2020 and December 2025, the US saw a record-breaking 26 percent inflation rate—one of the highest in modern history.[42] In practical terms, that means you would have needed a 26 percent raise during that period just to maintain the same spending power you had before the pandemic. And realistically, even a raise slightly above that would have been necessary to feel any improvement in your day-to-day finances.

For those who didn't receive a full 26 percent increase, the result was essentially the same as taking a pay cut. While your paycheck might have stayed the same—or even gone up a little—the cost of rent, groceries, and utilities continued to climb, leaving many households financially worse off than they were just a few years earlier. What makes this sting even more is that much of it was avoidable. Many corporations saw record profits during this time but shared far less of those gains with employees than they could have.[43]

From January 2020 through 2024, corporate after-tax profits rose by nearly 60 percent, the combined wealth of US billionaires increased by roughly 88 percent, and the wealthiest 1 percent saw its total net worth grow by about $16 trillion.[44] All the while, wage growth for typical workers has lagged far behind, contributing to a widening wealth gap that leaves most Americans further behind while those at the top capture the majority of economic gains.

This isn't a glitch in the system—it *is* the system. For decades, profits have been prioritized over people, and everyday Americans have been left to shoulder the cost. With the immense wealth this country generates, there's no reason we can't have billionaires, a thriving middle class, and virtually no poverty. The resources are there; what's lacking is the will to distribute them more fairly. Instead, corporate greed dominates, leaving millions of hardworking Americans barely scraping by on salaries that, just a decade ago, would have provided a comfortable life.

If you have to make $150,000 just to feel like you're getting ahead in this country—and most jobs only pay $40,000 to $60,000—it just doesn't add up. We've created a system where living paycheck to paycheck isn't a failure; it's the default.

And it's starting to show.

The US birth rate hit its lowest point since the 1970s in 2023.[45] Why? Because people can't afford to have kids. In a poll I ran on Instagram, nearly 67 percent of people who want children said they're putting it off solely because of finances and a lack of hope for the future. They're not afraid of being parents—they're afraid of being *poor* parents. That's heartbreaking.

And then we wonder why people feel burned out, hopeless, or disconnected.

When every day is just clocking in, clocking out, and watching your paycheck evaporate into bills, it's like running a marathon where the finish line keeps moving farther away. You keep pushing, keep grinding, keep sacrificing time with family and friends—yet you're still one unexpected expense away from falling behind. That kind of grind with no reward? That's what causes burnout. It's not the work—it's the lack of progress.

I saw a TikTok from a woman in her late twenties—a lawyer—who makes $80,000 a year, lives with her boyfriend, and still has two roommates just to make ends meet. That's a high-achieving, full-time professional . . . sharing a kitchen with two other adults.

That's not financial stability. That's economic limbo.

We've confused basic security for luxury. A one-bedroom apartment, a reliable car, a modest vacation once a year, a couple of pets, and a little savings shouldn't be considered "making it"—it should be normal. It should be the floor, not the ceiling.

Instead, we've built an economy where happiness feels like a luxury good.

So what happens next? We're already seeing it:

- Adult children living at home until twenty-five or thirty
- College grads with roommates well into their thirties

- Couples delaying marriage, kids, and homeownership indefinitely

It's reduced an entire generation to economic workers—just here to pay for a place to sleep, a car to get to work, and health insurance in case we break. That's not life. That's a trap. And it needs to change—because security, dignity, and joy shouldn't be luxuries reserved for the top 10 percent. They should be the minimum standard for everyone who gives their time, energy, and labor to keep this country running.

WHAT CAN BE DONE?

It's easy to feel powerless in the face of all this, but there are ways to fight back. Some states have started indexing minimum wage to inflation—so pay automatically rises as costs go up. Others are exploring profit-sharing models, where workers get a slice of the success they help create. And there's growing momentum for revitalizing unions, which have historically been one of the strongest tools for securing fair pay.

We're not asking for handouts. We're asking for our fair share of the productivity boom we helped create. If we're working harder and producing more than ever, why shouldn't our paychecks reflect that?

And the urgency here? It's now. Within a decade—if not sooner—AI and robotics will reshape almost every industry. Even if workers aren't replaced outright, corporations will see another massive productivity boom. And if history repeats itself, those profits will once again flow to the top while wages stay frozen, widening the already massive income gap.

We've already seen what happens when corporations write the

rules unchecked. Do we really want to wait until we're competing with robots to demand our fair share?

Because if the next generation is already buried under student debt before they even start their careers, they won't just be running on the treadmill—they'll be running on it in quicksand.

Chapter 4

THE COLLEGE DEBT TRAP

It feels like yesterday for many millennials and older Gen Zers— the constant drumbeat that *college was the only way to succeed*. I still remember the pressure as if it were 2006. It wasn't just that college was encouraged—it was that *not* going was framed as a guaranteed failure.

That's the narrative we need to change. I'm not pro college or anti college. I'm anti the idea that if you skip college, you're destined to fail. In today's world, that's simply not true. Technology has opened up more ways to earn a living than ever before. Blue-collar jobs are in high demand. Starting a business is more accessible. You can research hundreds of career paths from your phone—and many pay well without requiring a four-year degree.

That narrative didn't come out of nowhere. A few decades ago, college really *was* the move. It was far more affordable, and the jobs you landed afterward were much more likely to pay a premium for your degree. For many in previous generations, a college diploma was almost a guaranteed ticket to the middle class. But times have changed. The cost of college has skyrocketed, wages for many degree-required jobs have stagnated, and the job market itself has shifted. The old advice, while well-intentioned, no longer fits today's economic reality.

If someone chooses college, that's great—but we need a system and a national conversation that prepares young adults to make that decision wisely. That means understanding how student loans and interest actually work, recognizing the debt trap of tens (or hundreds) of thousands of dollars, and realistically forecasting life after graduation. What will your starting salary be? Where will you live? What will your expenses look like? And—critically—how long will it take to pay it all off?

We also need to talk about opportunity cost. For some, college is absolutely the right path—whether for career goals, passion, or the experience itself. For others, skipping it and starting work right away might be smarter. The good news, and something we should normalize: If you're unsure, it's okay to wait. Try different things, build skills, and if you decide to go to college at twenty-two, twenty-five, or even thirty—that's okay too.

For many millennials and Gen Zers, who've already gone to college, that choice is already behind us. We've paid our dues—literally—and some of us are living with the consequences. But if we don't take a hard look at how the system has changed, we risk sending the next generation straight into the same financial trap. And let's be honest—starting adult life at twenty-three with $100,000 in debt and a $52,000 salary is not exactly a head start.

But you can't blame us for wanting the college experience. Back then, it wasn't just part of the national conversation—it was baked into pop culture. The movies we grew up with painted college as a rite of passage, the place where you'd discover who you were and set the course for the rest of your life.

- *Good Will Hunting* made it seem like college was where you'd find intellectual purpose.
- *The Perfect Score* framed it as an elite club that determined your entire future.
- *Van Wilder* and *Old School* made it look like the best years of your life were waiting on campus.

- *Legally Blonde* told us that degrees meant prestige, money, and respect.

The message was loud and clear: Go to college, get the degree, land the high-paying job, and enjoy the good life. The alternative? Pursuing a trade, chasing a dream in the arts, or working a low-wage job and scraping by forever.

College was sold to us as the golden ticket. But for many, that ticket came with a pair of golden handcuffs.

THE FIRST TIME I QUESTIONED THE COLLEGE NARRATIVE

When I decided to move to Los Angeles after high school, my parents supported me. But I'll never forget the sheer panic in the eyes of some of my friends' parents when they learned I wasn't enrolling in college.

"How will you support yourself?" they asked.

"Is this a gap year?" they said. "You're going back to school eventually, right?"

They weren't being mean—they were genuinely worried for my future. To them, skipping college, to pursue an acting career, meant I'd be living in my parents' basement until I was forty. That's how deeply the "college or bust" idea was embedded.

But here's the thing—it's not our parents' fault.

For boomers and older Gen Xers, college actually worked. A four-year degree often cost $5,000–$10,000, and the salary boost was undeniable. In the 1980s, college graduates could expect to earn significantly more than their non-degree peers. Back then, the math checked out. So what changed? How did this fantastic stepping stone of education and opportunity turn into one of the biggest financial traps of our time?

THE GREAT PULLBACK: STATES CUT COLLEGE FUNDING

For our parents' and grandparents' generations, public universities weren't run like businesses—they were run like public infrastructure, funded mostly by the state. That's why they were called *state* schools. Legislatures paid most of the operating costs: professors, buildings, libraries, maintenance, the whole thing. Tuition wasn't meant to cover the real price of college; it was just a small contribution on top of what taxpayers already provided. Low tuition wasn't an accident. It was a policy choice.

Then, starting in the late 1970s and accelerating through the 1980s, that philosophy quietly changed. States stopped treating college as a public good and started treating it as a private investment. When budgets tightened, higher-ed funding was one of the first things to get cut. Universities didn't suddenly become wasteful—they just got handed a bill they used to share with the public.

So they did the only thing they could: they raised tuition.

Over the next few decades, states paid a smaller and smaller share of the cost of running public universities, while students and families were forced to cover more and more of it. The price of college didn't explode because education became more valuable—it exploded because the government stopped picking up the tab and shifted the cost onto young people and debt.

FROM AID TO LOANS: THE FEDERAL SWITCH

In the 1970s and early 1980s, low-income students could rely on Pell Grants to cover as much as 70 percent of the cost of attending a public university. These were actual grants, money you didn't have to pay back, designed to give low-income families and working-class families a real shot at college.

Today, Pell covers less than 30 percent. And as that support shrank, the government in the '80s and '90s shifted away from grants and leaned into student loans. Instead of giving students money to attend, they told them to borrow it.[46]

The message to colleges was basically: "Don't worry about keeping tuition affordable—students can just take out loans."

That single shift opened the floodgates. Colleges realized they could keep raising prices, because students would just go into debt for it.

THE 1992 HIGHER ED ACT: THE BLANK-CHECK ERA

In 1992, Congress passed amendments that created Direct PLUS Loans and expanded unsubsidized Stafford Loans.

Translation: Almost anyone could borrow, even to attend for-profit colleges and outrageously overpriced programs. And since loan approval was practically guaranteed, there was no real check on what schools could charge.

Colleges saw it and thought: "Wait, there's no cap? And students are guaranteed to get approved?"

You know what happened next—tuition went up. And up again. And again.

COLLEGE BECOMES A BUSINESS

By the late '90s and into the '00s, universities began running themselves less like schools and more like corporations. Administrative hiring outpaced faculty hiring, with the number of non-teaching staff growing by roughly 60 percent between 1993 and 2009.[47] At the same time, campuses poured money into luxury dorms, high-end gyms, and million-dollar stadiums, while spending on branding, marketing, and prestige accelerated.[48] Education increasingly took a back seat to scaling the brand.

NO RULES. NO CAPS. NO LIMITS.

There's no regulation that says a school can't charge $60,000 a year. No law says tuition has to match the value of the degree. And because student loans are federally backed, schools take no financial risk if graduates can't pay.

If you drop out? If your degree doesn't get you a job?

The government still gets paid, and the college still gets your tuition.

And what did all this create?

Well, let's compare the numbers for average in-state tuition and fees at public four-year colleges and student debt levels from then to now.

Year	Average Public Tuition	Average Student Debt
1979–1980	~$738–$900[49]	<$4,000
2024–2025	$11,000+[50]	~$37,000

As we see, college costs have exploded—faster than inflation, faster than wages, faster than housing. Millions are now carrying debt they can't escape, even decades after graduation.

It's not that college has no value. It's that we turned education into a business . . . and students into customers forced to borrow for a ticket in. And these policy decisions have led to a student loan debt crisis that has surpassed $1.7 trillion.

THE $1.7 TRILLION ANCHOR

That's not just a big number; it's the size of another country's entire economy. In fact, it's roughly equal to the GDP of Canada. Imagine an entire nation's yearly output—every product, every service, every paycheck—owed in the form of student loans.

If that $1.7 trillion were a company, it would be one of the largest on Earth—bigger than Amazon, bigger than Google. But unlike those companies, this "business" doesn't innovate, hire workers, or create anything tangible. It simply collects payments, month after month, year after year, siphoning wealth from the people who were told this debt was the key to a better life.

Now, for some people, that deal still works. If you know exactly what you want to do, your career pays well, and you've run the numbers ahead of time, a degree can absolutely be a launchpad. Doctors, engineers, specialized attorneys—these fields often require formal education, and the return on investment can still be strong.

But here's the danger: For millions of others, the math doesn't work out—not because they were lazy or failed to "hustle," but because the cost of higher education has skyrocketed far beyond what starting salaries can support.

The average graduate today carries a $536 monthly payment stretched out over twenty years.[51] That's more than $6,000 a year. Over the life of the loan, that's more than $120,000 in after-tax income—often double the original loan amount, with tens of thousands of dollars going entirely to interest.

That's $120,000 that could have:

- Been a massive down payment for a starter home;
- Covered the cost of raising a child for their first decade;
- Doubled your retirement savings if invested in an index fund.

Instead, it's going to a bill for a degree that, in too many cases, isn't delivering the financial return people were promised.

This isn't just about individual budgets—it's shaping the whole economy. Every dollar going to student loan payments is a dollar *not* spent at local businesses, *not* invested in new startups, *not* circulating to stimulate growth. It's money that could be fueling the economy but is instead locked up in a debt cycle designed to benefit lenders.

Even Barack and Michelle Obama—yes, the former president and first lady—were still paying off student loans in their forties. As Obama once said, "Our student loans cost more than our mortgage."[52]

Miss a payment, and you're not just dealing with late fees. Your credit score tanks. Your interest rate on future loans jumps. You might even lose out on job opportunities, because, yes, some employers check your credit.

This isn't just debt. It's a generational anchor. And unless we cut the chain, we'll keep dragging it through every major life decision—where we live, what we buy, and how we plan for the future. I spoke with Hannah Maruyama, coauthor of *The Degree Free Way*, on *The Freddie Smith Podcast*. She introduced me to a piece of the puzzle I hadn't seen before. A portion of that $1.7 trillion student debt has a secret lurking in the shadows—and if it's not addressed, it could turn into a full-blown crisis: Some student loans are being sliced up, packaged, and sold to investors—similar to the risky mortgages that triggered the 2008 financial crisis.[53] Only this time, there's no house to seize if things go wrong. The "collateral" is your future income. Which means the debt crisis isn't just a burden we carry—it's become a profit center for Wall Street. We talk about the 2008 crisis like it was a once-in-a-lifetime event—a freak storm of bad loans, risky bets, and unchecked greed. But what if I told you history is repeating itself right now? Only this time, it's not homes being foreclosed—it's people's futures.

In 2008, banks handed out subprime mortgages like candy to people who didn't fully understand the terms. Then, those mortgages were bundled into investment products called *mortgage-backed securities* and sold off to investors. The logic? If people defaulted, the bank could just seize the house. When the bubble popped, millions lost their homes, their savings, and their shot at a stable life.

Fast-forward to today.

Now, it's not homes being bundled—it's student loans.

That's right: Banks and financial institutions package up student debt and sell it off as student loan asset-backed securities (SLABS) to investors. The big difference? If borrowers can't pay, there's no house to take. No physical asset. Just the borrower's future income.

And here's the terrifying part: Federal student loans are nearly impossible to erase in bankruptcy. You're required to prove *undue hardship* in court—a step few can afford. That means if you take on $100,000 in loans and life goes sideways, there's often no reset button. You're carrying that scorecard for ten, twenty, even thirty years.

Default doesn't result in a foreclosure—it results in financial consequences that can follow you forever. The government can garnish your wages, intercept your tax refunds, and even withhold up to 15 percent of your Social Security.

The reason Wall Street loves student loans is simple: They're backed not by a home but by your future income. And because they know most borrowers won't be able to escape them, they're considered "safe" investments. That's why they're overpaying for these loan bundles. The risk of default is technically low—not because people can afford the debt, but because for a lot of borrowers, there's no way out.

The irony? These loans are often handed out to seventeen- and eighteen-year-olds who, in many cases, barely understand compound interest, let alone what it means to be on the hook for six figures before they even set foot in their first real job. No financial education in high school. No legal counsel. Just a signature and a lifetime of payments.

At least with the housing collapse, you could lose the home and eventually move on. But with student loans? There's nothing to repossess—only decades of forced payments and broken dreams.

We didn't fix the system.

We just changed the product.

And once again, bad policies have left millennials and Gen Zers holding the bag.

THE LAST RISK TO CONSIDER AND PLAN FOR

Imagine you're a first-year college student—bright-eyed, full of ambition. You spend four (maybe six) years grinding through classes, racking up student loan debt, and finally walking across that stage to grab your diploma. But by the time you step into the workforce . . . the job you trained for is already disappearing.

This isn't some far-fetched conspiracy—it's happening right now. Automation, AI, rapid tech advancements, and offshoring are wiping out entire fields faster than universities can update their course catalogs.

A decade ago, no one thought accounting was at risk. Today, AI software can do in seconds what once took accountants hours. Law firms are replacing entry-level paralegals with algorithms that can sift through thousands of legal documents before you've finished your morning coffee. Marketing teams, journalists, even graphic designers are now competing with AI that can create content at scale and for pennies on the dollar.

And it's not just "creative" or "white-collar" jobs. I was at my niece's sixth birthday party recently, chatting with a family friend who's a primary care physician. Nine years of schooling. Hundreds of thousands in loans. A decade of sacrifice. You'd think that kind of investment guaranteed career security. But when I asked how the future looked for his profession, he didn't hesitate:

"With the way things are going," he said, "I don't know how much longer my job will even exist in the way it does now."

He explained how telemedicine and AI are already diagnosing conditions more accurately than some doctors. For now, he loves the tech—it saves him time. But he can see the writing on the wall: Insurance companies and healthcare systems will always look for ways to cut costs, and replacing people with machines is cheaper.

If even medicine isn't immune, what does that mean for everyone else?

Meanwhile, colleges keep selling degrees for careers that might be extinct in ten years—leaving graduates with $80,000 in debt and no job security. It's like buying a brand-new car, only to find out it's been discontinued the moment you drive it off the lot. And the truth is, universities don't care. They'll keep taking tuition checks while letting students figure out the fallout.

And that's just the job market. The other wild card? *You.*

When I was in school, I wanted to be an actor. That was the plan. But today? I run my own brand, host a podcast, and create content for a living—a career path that didn't even exist when I was in high school. Whole industries can emerge in a single decade, and just as many can disappear.

We also evolve as people. You might love teaching for fifteen years, then want to switch careers at thirty-five. You might thrive in marketing, then feel pulled toward something new at forty-five. You might even start a completely new career at sixty-five. That's normal. But if you're shackled by massive student debt, making a change can feel impossible.

That's the real trap: Debt limits your ability to pivot. And in a world moving this fast, the ability to pivot might be your most valuable asset.

At the end of the day, most young people don't want to be rich for the sake of being rich—they want *freedom.* Freedom to pursue opportunities without being weighed down by a decision they made at eighteen. Freedom to chase a new dream without doing the math on whether they can still make their loan payment.

So before signing up for $100,000 in debt, ask yourself: Do I want to bet my future on a career that might not exist—or that I might not even want—ten years from now?

Because in this economy, your best career move might be staying financially nimble enough to grab the opportunities that don't even exist yet.

That's why it's important to understand these examples, because everything I just laid out represents the risk you're taking when you sign your name on a student loan agreement. And yet, for many people, college and loans are still the right move.

According to a 2011 analysis, the average bachelor's degree holder earns about $1 million more over their lifetime than someone with only a high school diploma.[54] The research itself is sound, but the way this figure is often interpreted tells only part of the story.

That number can be heavily inflated by high-paying careers in STEM, business, and finance. Remove those fields from the equation, and the lifetime earnings gap can shrink dramatically—sometimes to the point where the extra income barely outweighs the debt.

It's the same illusion we see when people talk about the "average" US salary, which sits around $60,000 a year. That average is pulled upward by very high earners, while the median—the number that reflects what a typical worker actually makes—is much lower. In reality, most workers earn around $46,000 a year, or roughly the low-$20s per hour. The gap exists because a relatively small number of ultra-high incomes skew the math.

And so, in one of the richest countries in the world, we've reached a bizarre crossroads: It can feel like you have to choose between following your passion and earning a paycheck big enough to survive. If college were still affordable like it once was, that choice wouldn't feel so brutal. But this is the reality we live in. So the question becomes: What do you do?

PASSION VERSUS PAYCHECKS

Money isn't everything. Loving what you do matters. If you have a deep passion for teaching, social work, or the arts, you might willingly take the financial hit because the work itself fulfills you. There's value in waking up excited about your job.

But passion won't always keep the lights on.

Believe me, I get it. Pursuing an acting career is one of the hardest paths you can take if financial stability is a priority. I was one of the lucky ones who somehow managed to make a career out of my passion, but it didn't come without hardships or moments when I seriously considered quitting. I even have friends who are more "famous" than me—actors with massive resumes—who make a ton of money one year and then struggle to even qualify for health insurance the next.

That's what life is about, though—taking calculated risks and trying to thread the needle between passion and paycheck.

If you choose purpose over paychecks, you need a bulletproof plan to manage student debt. Because even if you love your job, you still have to eat—and unfortunately, many "passion careers" leave people financially drowning if you don't prepare properly. There was a time when going to college didn't require financial bravery. You could take out a small loan, graduate, get a job you enjoyed, and still afford rent, groceries, and a little savings. But that world is gone.

Since 1980, the cost of public college has soared by more than 1,300 percent in nominal terms, climbing from about $800 a year to more than $11,000 for in-state tuition.[55] Nothing else in American life has risen that fast—not housing, not gas, not groceries, not wages.

In 1980, a minimum-wage worker earning $3.10 an hour needed about 290 hours of work to cover a year of in-state tuition. That's roughly two months of full-time work; a summer job could realistically pay for college.

Today? Even someone earning *double* the federal minimum wage—$14.50 an hour—would need to work more than 750 hours to pay for a year of tuition. That's nearly five months of full-time work for *just* tuition, with nothing left for housing, food, books, or fees.

This is why working your way through college without debt is far harder today. The student's effort hasn't changed—the economy has.

And what's wild is that degrees no longer guarantee the stability they once did. Students pay exponentially more for an outcome that's far less certain.

The promise of a secure, high-paying job? For many, it's broken.

For the lucky ones—those who graduate into careers that match their training and pay enough to manage their debt—the payoff is worth celebrating.

But for others—those who drop out or graduate only to end up underemployed—the reality is painful. Especially when there's a heavy debt burden attached. Today, about 40 percent of recent graduates work in jobs that don't require a degree, a trend hitting Gen Z the hardest.[56]

But the most frustrating story is the one so many millennials know too well: You finish four to six years of college, land a job in your field, and realize the paycheck barely covers rent and your student loan interest—let alone allows you to get ahead.

THE TEACHER WHO QUIT FOR THE BEACH BAR

A few months ago, my wife and I took a staycation in Clearwater, Florida. While sipping drinks at a beach bar, I struck up a conversation with the bartender. He was really good at explaining things—teacher-level good.

Turns out, he *was* a teacher.

For years, he worked full time in education, clocking fifty-hour weeks and barely scraping by. To make ends meet, he bartended on weekends. One day, he ran the numbers and realized that working just Fridays and Saturdays behind the bar paid more than his teaching salary.

So he made a radical choice: He quit teaching altogether.

Now? He works four days a week serving mai tais on the beach and earns more than $100,000 a year—nearly double what he made as a teacher.

Of course, not everyone can—or should—abandon their career for bartending. But the fact that a former educator (who loved what he did) makes more money serving tequila shots than shaping young minds should tell us something: The system isn't just flawed. It's upside down.

The bartender and teacher story isn't just about underpaying hard-working people—it's about what those jobs represent: careers that require years of education, tens of thousands of dollars in loans, and yet can still leave people struggling to get by.

And here's where things get messy: Most people don't even fully understand the *rules of the game* before they borrow. We sign our names at eighteen, take the money, and assume we'll just "pay it back later." But student loans have a way of quietly growing in the background like financial mold, and by the time you realize it's spreading . . . it's everywhere.

Chapter 5

HOW STUDENT LOANS WORK (THE STUFF THEY DON'T TELL YOU)

When it comes to paying for college, there are two main types of loans: *federal* and *private*.

Think of *federal loans* like borrowing from a stubborn but predictable relative—the rules are the same for everyone, interest rates are usually lower, and there are built-in safety nets like income-driven repayment plans or potential loan forgiveness.

- **When they make sense:** If you have little to no credit history (most eighteen-year-olds), want access to flexible repayment options, or plan to work in public service where forgiveness programs may apply.
- **Example:** You're a student from a middle-class family, no cosigner available, and you qualify for subsidized loans (where the government covers interest while you're in school).

Private loans, on the other hand, are more like borrowing from a corporate loan shark in a suit—they can have variable interest rates, fewer repayment protections, and little sympathy if you lose your job or fall behind.

- **When they make sense:** You've maxed out your federal loan limit but still have a gap to cover, you have excellent credit (or a creditworthy cosigner), and you can secure a competitive fixed rate.
- **Example:** Your tuition is $40,000 a year, you've borrowed the max $12,500 in federal loans, but you still need $27,500 to fill the gap—so you shop for the best private rate.

Some students use both, starting with federal loans (to lock in the protections) and filling the rest with private loans.

SUBSIDIZED VERSUS UNSUBSIDIZED—A HUGE DIFFERENCE

Here's a detail that can save you thousands: *Subsidized loans* don't build interest while you're in school (or during certain deferment periods) because the government is covering it for you. This is the best-case scenario.

- **Who qualifies?** Subsidized loans are only available to undergraduates and are based on *financial need*, determined by your FAFSA (Free Application for Federal Student Aid).
- If your family's income and assets are too high, you might not qualify.

Unsubsidized loans, however, start racking up interest the moment the money is disbursed—even while you're still in school. The interest you don't pay gets added to your balance, so you end up paying interest on top of interest (known as capitalization).

- **Who qualifies?** Pretty much anyone enrolled at least half-time, undergrad or grad, regardless of financial need.

Think of it like this:

- **Subsidized** = The government babysits your interest for a while.
- **Unsubsidized** = Your interest is like a meter in a taxi—running nonstop from day one, whether you're riding or not.

"YOU DON'T HAVE TO PAY UNTIL YOU GRADUATE"—THE LIE OF COMFORT

Here's where most people with unsubsidized federal and/or private loans get into trouble. The sales pitch they give you: "Don't worry! You don't have to make payments until six months after graduation."

Sounds great . . . until you realize interest never took that same vacation.

Take Sarah. She borrowed $40,000 in unsubsidized federal loans over four years. She thought, "No problem—I'll just start paying after I graduate." But the interest had other plans. At a 5 percent rate, that's about $2,000 a year in interest alone. Four years later, Sarah walked across the stage with her diploma . . . and a balance of more than $48,000.

That's thousands more she never *used*. It's just the cost of time passing.

DAILY INTEREST: THE SILENT ENEMY

Here's where it gets even sneakier: Interest often accrues daily. Every. Single. Day.

If your minimum payment is $250 and your monthly interest is $230, then $230 is just treading water—only $20 actually touches the principal. That's why so many people on TikTok post stories like this:

"I borrowed $80,000 for school. I've been paying for fifteen years. I've paid over $100,000 so far . . . and I still owe $90,000."

It's not bad math. It's just the reality of how these loans are structured. If you only cover interest (or barely more), the principal doesn't budge. And if your loans are on a twenty- or twenty-five-year plan, that's decades of your life in debt for a degree you finished before Facebook went public.

THE REAL COST OF AN UNSUBSIDIZED LOAN (DO THE MATH BEFORE YOU SIGN)

Let's use Sarah's story to dig into the math here and see how that debt really behaves.

She took out *$40,000 in unsubsidized federal loans* at a 5 percent interest rate.

STEP 1: FIGURE OUT THE INTEREST WHILE IN SCHOOL

Unsubsidized loans start building interest the moment the money hits your account. Interest accrues daily, but for simplicity, here's the yearly math:

Year 1:
Loan balance = $40,000
Interest (5 percent) = $2,000
New balance = $42,000

Year 2:
Loan balance = $42,000
Interest (5 percent) = $2,100
New balance = $44,100

Year 3:
Loan balance = $44,100
Interest (5 percent) = $2,205
New balance = $46,305

Year 4:
Loan balance = $46,305
Interest (5 percent) = $2,315.25
New balance = $48,620.25

STEP 2: UNDERSTAND CAPITALIZATION

That $8,620.25 in interest isn't just sitting off to the side, it gets added to Sarah's balance (capitalized). Now, any future interest will be calculated on *$48,620.25* moving forward, not $40,000. This is the debt snowball effect working *against* her, and quite possibly you if you're in the same boat.

STEP 3: SEE WHAT YOUR MONTHLY PAYMENT WILL REALLY BE

On the standard ten-year repayment plan, a $48,620.25 current balance at 5 percent equals about a $515.69 monthly payment.

First Month:
Interest: $202.59
Principal: $313.10

After One Year of Payments:
Total paid: $6,188.28 (12 × $515.69)

Interest paid: $2,368.65
Principal paid: $3,819.63
Remaining balance: $44,800.62

Even after a year of faithfully paying more than $500 a month, Sarah has chipped away less than $4,000 from the principal—the rest has gone to interest. So how much did that $40,000 student loan actually cost?

HOW IT BREAKS DOWN

If Sarah consistently makes the standard $515.69 payment each month:

- **Principal:** $40,000 (the amount actually borrowed)
- **Interest accrued while in school:** $8,620.25 (because it was unsubsidized)
- **Interest during ten-year repayment:** $13,262.55
- **Total interest over life of loan:** $21,882.80
- **Final total paid:** $61,882.80

This means that in order to borrow $40,000 of unsubsidized loans for school, she'll actually spend nearly *$62,000* repaying it. More than *half* of the extra $22K is just interest for the privilege of using that money. So here is how to mitigate some of that burden.

HOW TO KEEP THE INTEREST MONSTER FROM GROWING

You can't change the rules of the loan, but you can play the game smarter. Here are five steps you can take to get ahead of the student loan snowball.

1. PAY INTEREST WHILE IN SCHOOL

Even $50 a month toward interest while you're still in class can save thousands later.

2. EXTRA PRINCIPAL PAYMENTS

When you pay more than the minimum, specify that it should go toward *principal*, not future interest. That way, you cut the root of the problem—and future interest is calculated on a smaller balance.

3. BIWEEKLY PAYMENTS

Split your monthly payment into two smaller payments every two weeks. This slightly reduces average daily principal and chips away at interest faster.

4. REFINANCE CAREFULLY

If you have stable income and a good credit score, refinancing to a lower interest rate can be a game changer—just be careful not to lose federal protections you might need later.

5. WINDFALL ATTACKS

Tax refund? Bonus? Side hustle income? Throw chunks at your principal. Every dollar you remove today is interest you *never* have to pay in the future.

FROM LOAN MATH TO REAL LIFE

Now that you know the *true* cost of your loan and what your monthly payment will be, you can reverse engineer your post-college budget before you even step foot on campus. This isn't about scaring yourself out of going—it's about walking in with your eyes wide open.

Here are some key questions to ask yourself when picking a career path and deciding where to live after graduation:

- What will be my *starting salary* in my chosen field?
- What will my *take-home pay* be after taxes, 401(k) contributions, and health insurance?
- Where do I want to live, and what does housing cost there *today*?
- What will my salary look like *five years in*?
- Does that growth path fit the lifestyle I actually want?

Equipped with this knowledge, Emily has decided to take a different path than Sarah.

Emily is eighteen and wants to become a marketing manager. She takes out $40,000 in unsubsidized loans for a four-year degree. She runs the math like we did earlier and sees the real price tag—about *$62,000* over ten years. She's fine with that and she writes the $515/month loan payment into her future budget.

She does her homework and finds that in Florida, an entry-level marketing role pays around $60,000 a year. After taxes and 401(k) contributions, her monthly take-home pay will be about $4,000.

She subtracts the $515 for student loans and is left with $3,485. Now she hops on Zillow to check apartments in the city she wants to work in. This gives her a real sense of whether her budget matches her dream lifestyle.

By doing this math *before* she enrolls, Emily can:

- Decide if she's comfortable with her starting lifestyle;
- Set realistic expectations for her first job;
- Figure out how much she should aim to earn during college from part-time work to start off even stronger.

This kind of planning doesn't kill the dream—it builds a runway for it. Instead of being blindsided by bills after graduation, you're already in control.

If you're reading this in your twenties, thirties, or forties and you're already deep in student loans, I didn't forget about you! You're not doomed to be paying these off until retirement. But you *do* need a strategy that goes beyond "just make the minimum payment and hope for the best."

Here are a few realistic options to start tilting the game in your favor:

1. MAKE EXTRA PRINCIPAL PAYMENTS

Even an extra $50–$100/month toward your loan's **principal** can save you thousands in interest over the life of the loan. Think of it like this: Every dollar you put toward principal is a dollar that stops racking up rent in interest forever.

2. REFINANCE—BUT ONLY IF IT MAKES SENSE

If you've got solid credit and stable income, refinancing at a lower interest rate can be a game changer. But beware—refinancing federal loans into private loans means giving up protections like income-driven repayment and forgiveness programs. Run the numbers, then decide.

3. EXPLORE INCOME-DRIVEN REPAYMENT (IDR) PLANS

If your monthly payment is crushing you, federal IDR plans can lower it to a percentage of your discretionary income. It might mean paying longer, but it can free up breathing room in your budget so you can still save and invest.

4. ATTACK IT IN SPRINTS

Instead of aiming to "pay it all off someday," set mini goals—like killing one loan or $5,000 in principal over the next twelve months. Each sprint gives you momentum, motivation, and visible progress.

5. DON'T LET DEBT STALL YOUR WHOLE LIFE

Yes, student debt is a drag, but don't let it keep you from building wealth in other ways. Even while paying loans, put *something* toward retirement—compound interest is too powerful to wait until you're debt free.

You can't change the decision that got you the loans, but you can change the story from here on out. Whether you crush the debt aggressively or manage it strategically while investing elsewhere, the key is to get *intentional*—because debt without a plan is just financial quicksand.

To round out this chapter, I want to share an alternative path as a thought experiment. In earlier chapters we considered how the middle-class experience has been undercut by rising costs and other factors. We looked at just how twenty dollars an hour doesn't go as far these days. We examined skyrocketing housing costs and the trap of 401(k)s versus pension vehicles more frequently available to prior generations. And now we've seen the real cost of college playing out in examples.

There are several paths forward where you don't have to be steamrolled by the system. The following is one of my favorites. It's not easy, but it is powerful if you can accomplish it. It'll also give you some insight on the power of compound interest.

THE ROAD TO A MULTIMILLION-DOLLAR RETIREMENT

Earlier, we touched on careers that could help someone earn millions more over a lifetime than going straight into work after high school. But what if, instead of sprinting into college debt at eighteen, there's another path? An unconventional one—that could lead to the ultimate financial freedom.

Not a trust fund. Not a lottery ticket. Just a plan so simple it almost sounds too good to be true: a path where an average American kid could retire with around *$5 million* while working a regular job.

Sounds wild, right? I even shared this theory on social media, and it caught the attention of MarketWatch. They published an article on it and brought in financial experts to weigh in.[57] The verdict? The math works. Start early, invest consistently, and compound growth does the heavy lifting. But they were quick to point out why this isn't realistic for most families. I don't disagree that it would be difficult, but I *do* think it's a powerful alternative for some young people.

Here's how it works:

STEP 1: A CAR WITH A PURPOSE

At sixteen, your kid gets their first big financial responsibility: a reliable used car that'll last at least seven years—price tag around $12K. You cosign, and they get a part-time job bringing in $1,000–$1,200 a month.

The deal: $500 a month goes toward the car until it's paid off. The rest—$500 to $700—is theirs to enjoy or save. By graduation, the car is *theirs* outright.

Milestone one: They own an asset, debt free, with no interest paid. Cool . . . but where's the $5 million? That's next.

STEP 2: THREE YEARS OF FOCUS (AGES EIGHTEEN TO TWENTY-ONE)

Instead of racing into college with an $80K loan for a degree they may not even want, they stay home for three years. You cover the basics—rent, food, utilities—and they work full time (and maybe pick up a side hustle), earning around $35K a year.

The arrangement:

- They keep $10K a year for themselves.
- They invest the other $25K into a simple S&P 500 index fund.

Three years later, they've invested *$75K*. With compounding and reinvested dividends, that's roughly *$80K* by age twenty-one.

And here's the magic: Without ever adding another dime (beyond reinvesting dividends), that $80K, earning an 8 percent annual return, could grow into about *$4 million* when they are seventy.

Let's pause to compare how these kids are doing before we move on to step 3.

At twenty-one, your kid has:

- A paid-off car;
- Zero debt;
- $80K compounding in the market.

Their "traditional path" friend has:

- $60K in student loans;
- $20K in car payments;
- $5K in credit card debt;

One is building wealth. The other is digging out before they can even start.

STEP 3: BUILDING A LIFE ON THEIR TERMS

At twenty-one, they move out, maybe making $40K–$50K (and eventually $60K–$80K later in their career). Instead of scrambling to catch up on retirement savings most of their lives, they get to enjoy the journey.

Because their retirement is secured early, they have options:

- Lease the car they want;
- Rent the apartment they love;
- Take career risks;
- Spend on experiences.

If they choose to go to college later, start a business, or travel the world, they can—without wrecking their financial future.

THE HARSH TRUTH ABOUT WAITING

Most people don't get serious about retirement until their thirties or forties. I know because I was one of them. My wife and I didn't start investing until our mid-thirties—even after earning a lot in my twenties, I'm sad to report we never invested a single dollar into the stock market or real estate, and by the time we figured out the power of compounding interest, we were nearly $200K in debt. We had to dig out of that mess first before we could even start investing. Now we are years behind and trying our best to catch up.

If you start at thirty-five and want the same $4 million by seventy, you'd need to invest a whopping *$1,740/month*—around $730K (plus reinvesting dividends) for thirty-five years.

Compare that to the twenty-one-year-old who only had to invest $75K (plus reinvesting dividends).

That's the power of starting early.

THE REAL QUESTION

For those who still have this option, ask yourself: Would you rather delay "starting life" from ages eighteen to twenty-one, work your ass off to invest $75K before your twenty-first birthday—or start at thirty-five and have to invest more than $700K to reach the same result by age seventy?

This isn't going to be the game plan for everyone. It's a thought experiment to show the raw power of compound interest. The example I gave is extreme, but the takeaway is simple: What variation of this plan could you commit to, regardless of your age?

The truth is that we can't afford to delay retirement any longer. Every year we wait, every impulse purchase we choose over investing, every piece of "bad debt"—car leases, high-interest credit cards, personal loans—pushes that goal further away.

Because at the end of the day, what does our generation really want?

Not yachts and private jets—but financial freedom.

Freedom to explore new ideas.

Freedom to take risks.

Freedom to change direction when life throws curveballs.

Whether or not you go to college, having a retirement plan in place gives you the power to thrive and the flexibility to pivot in an ever-changing world. That's the real win.

We've seen the challenges individuals face when debt isn't managed well, but zoom out, and the student debt crisis isn't just about people drowning in payments. It's a reflection of a bigger pattern: America itself has been running on debt, borrowing against tomorrow to paper over today. The same way young people are saddled with decades of loan payments, our entire nation is carrying a tab that keeps getting kicked down the road. And just like with student loans, the people at the top keep cashing in while the rest of us shoulder the risk. Which raises the question: If student debt can reshape an entire generation's future, what happens when the debt belongs to an entire country?

Chapter 6

AMERICA'S BROKEN MONEY MACHINE

Most Americans, regardless of age, know the frustration of working your ass off forty or fifty hours a week only to open your paycheck and see it whittled down by deductions. Every year, Americans contribute about $4.9 trillion in taxes to the federal government. That's a ton of money.

Originally, those dollars were meant to fund things like the military, infrastructure, Social Security, Medicare, and welfare programs. And while that might sound good on paper, here's the problem: Our government doesn't stop at spending the $4.9 trillion we give it. Year after year, they overspend. The difference between what they take in and what they spend is called *the deficit*.

And how do they cover that gap? They borrow. Each time they do, it's like America pulling out an American Express card. Just like your credit card or student loan, that debt comes with interest. Only this time, we—taxpayers—are the ones footing the bill.

A few decades ago, our national debt was relatively manageable. Even then, some politicians were warning that borrowing couldn't go on forever. In 1992, independent presidential candidate Ross Perot famously cautioned, "We cannot spend our children's money. We are on the edge of a revolution of young people who are starting to realize that we, our generation, have put them four trillion in debt, and they don't like it, and they shouldn't."

So, what's happened since then? Did we pay it down? Did we at least cut it in half? Not even close. Instead, the debt has ballooned. Today, it sits at more than *$37 trillion*. And according to *The New York Times*, over the next decade, it's projected to hit *$54 trillion*.

Those numbers are so massive they almost stop feeling real. So let's bring it home. Imagine your retired parents racked up $370,000 in credit card debt on cruises, European vacations, and home renovations. In 2024, they tell you they're broke and need help. Out of love, you give them $49,000 to cover necessities. They cry, thank you, and swear you're the best kid in the world. But the very next year at Thanksgiving, they admit they blew through all your money, added another $62,000 in spending, and tacked on $15,000 more in credit card debt. And then they ask you—again—for $50,000.

That's basically the US government's relationship with taxpayers. Except in the family scenario, when the reckless parents die, the debt dies with them. With government debt, it doesn't disappear—it gets passed down to us and future generations.

In 2023 alone, out of the $4.5 trillion we paid in taxes, nearly $1 trillion went just to cover the *interest* on that debt.

US Government	**Parent Analogy**
Total Debt: $37 Trillion	$370,000
Total Revenue: $4.9 Trillion	$49,000
Total Spending: $6.2 Trillion	$62,000
Annual Debt Payment: $1 Trillion	$10,000

Paying interest on this mountain of debt is slowly eating everything else. We're busting our asses, handing over 20 percent or more of our paychecks, only to see a giant chunk wasted on debt payments. About 20 percent of federal revenue now goes to servicing debt we never signed off on. Another 54 percent is locked up in Social Security, Medicare, and defense. That leaves just scraps for everything else—veterans, education, infrastructure, innovation—the stuff that actually moves the country forward.

As individuals, if we skip a credit card payment, our credit score tanks. Miss taxes, and the IRS shows up at your door. But the government? They just keep borrowing. No one comes knocking. And when the bill is due, it's not them—it's us.

And here's where it gets even trickier: Unlike you and me, the government has another option on the table. When the debt piles up too high, they don't just borrow more—they can literally *print money*. But printing money comes with its own dangerous consequences . . .

THE DIFFERENCE BETWEEN GOVERNMENT DEBT AND PRINTING MONEY (QUANTITATIVE EASING)

All right, let's nerd out for a few minutes—because understanding how the government borrows money versus how the Federal Reserve prints money is one of the most important economic lessons no one ever bothered to teach us.

Both methods can have short-term benefits (or so they say), but ultimately, the combination of these two actions leads to the same outcome: inflation and the devaluation of our dollar.

And where does that extra money go?

Don't say it, Freddie.

. . . Fine, I'll say it.

The top 1 percent again.

Whenever you hear a politician pound their chest and brag about "slashing the deficit," you might think, *Wow, maybe they actually paid down some of our national debt!*

Nope.

What they actually mean is they were planning to borrow $2 trillion this year, but through their "careful" budgeting, they're only borrowing $1.7 trillion instead. They're still adding $1.7 trillion to our debt—just slightly less than expected.

Our government does this every single year.

We've normalized reckless spending to the point where we barely flinch when the national debt climbs past $37 trillion.

How do they borrow this money?

Through the US Treasury—which manages our hard-earned tax dollars and issues Treasury bonds to investors (both foreign and domestic). These bonds are essentially IOUs from the government, and when people or institutions buy them, they're lending money to Uncle Sam—who then spends it however Congress sees fit. Mind you, we don't get to vote on how that money is spent. Congress just passes bills, borrows money, and hands us the bill.

And this kind of borrowing should only be used for national emergencies, like the pandemic relief efforts that helped keep families and small businesses afloat.

But instead?

The government has become so addicted to borrowing that they spend an extra $1.5 trillion every single year—no emergency required.

And every time they do this?

Massive inflation. Devaluation of our dollar. And ordinary Americans footing the bill.

PRINTING MONEY: THE FEDERAL RESERVE'S FAVORITE MAGIC TRICK

Now, when people say the government is printing money, they don't mean there's a giant printer in DC spitting out hundred-dollar bills, with suitcases of cash getting dropped out of helicopters.

(Although, at this point, that wouldn't even surprise me.)

What's actually happening is this: The Federal Reserve—which acts as the central bank for commercial banks—creates money out of thin air and uses it to buy existing debts, like mortgage-backed securities or government bonds. This frees up money for banks, allowing them to loan out more, theoretically stimulating the economy.

The fancy economic term for this process?

Quantitative easing (QE).

But the simpler way to put it?

They're "printing money" without actually printing it. This manipulation of the free market benefits banks, corporations, and the wealthy, while creating inflation for the rest of us.

And here's what you need to remember: Inflation is just another form of taxation. If inflation rises by 3 percent in a year, that means your money loses 3 percent of its spending power. Even if you didn't get a tax hike, you're still losing money—just in a sneakier way. Here's the crazy part: Just like everything else, it wasn't always like this. A major reason we have out-of-control inflation is because we decided to leave the gold standard.

HOW WE DITCHED THE GOLD STANDARD—AND WHY IT CHANGED EVERYTHING

Let's take a trip back to August 15, 1971—the day President Richard Nixon made a decision that would change the financial future of every American.

That was the day the United States officially ditched the gold standard.

For most of modern history, the US dollar was backed by gold—meaning every paper bill in circulation represented actual gold stored in the US Treasury. If you wanted to, you could literally walk into a bank and exchange your paper money for gold.

Gold was the guardrail that kept governments from printing money recklessly, because every dollar printed had to be backed by something real—a tangible asset with intrinsic value. But in 1971, Nixon announced that the US would suspend the convertibility of dollars into gold, essentially cutting the final thread between the dollar and real value. And just like that, money became nothing more than an idea—a piece of paper we all agree has value, even though it's backed by nothing.

And what happened next?

Inflation skyrocketed.

WHY DID WE LEAVE THE GOLD STANDARD?

The official explanation was that it was necessary to stabilize the economy and prevent foreign governments from draining US gold reserves. But the real reason? The government wanted to spend more money than it actually had.

The Vietnam War, the Cold War, massive domestic spending programs—the US was burning through cash at an unsustainable rate. And because the dollar was pegged to gold, the government was limited in how much money it could print. By cutting ties with gold, the US gave itself permission to print unlimited money—whenever and however it wanted.

No more pesky limits. No more accountability. Just unlimited government spending at the expense of every working American. And what happens when you print endless amounts of money? Prices go up. Wages stagnate. And the dollar loses its buying power. Sound familiar?

IMAGINE IF STARBUCKS RAN THIS WAY

Let's put this in real-world terms.

Imagine you're a loyal Starbucks customer, racking up points on your rewards card. For every ten points you earn, you get a free drink. Simple, right? But then, one day, Starbucks announces: "Great news! We're printing an unlimited number of reward points for everyone! Free drinks for life!"

At first, this sounds incredible. You're thinking, *Hell yeah, I'm never paying for coffee again!* But then, reality sets in. Because everyone now has unlimited points, Starbucks quietly makes an adjustment.

Instead of needing ten points for a free drink, it now costs one hundred. Then two hundred. Then five hundred. Before you know it, your points are worthless.

That's exactly what happened when we left the gold standard.

By printing unlimited money, the government devalued the dollar, making it worth less and less over time. The money in your pocket didn't physically shrink, but what it could buy sure did. This is why the jaw-dropping stat from my introduction happened in the first place. That $100 bill from 1971? You'd need nearly $900 today to buy the same amount of goods—meaning the dollar has lost almost 90 percent of its purchasing power. And did the government print unlimited money over the past fifty years? Maybe not technically unlimited, but since then, the Federal Reserve has created nearly $9 trillion out of thin air—money that mostly flowed straight into Wall Street and the wealthy in some way or another, while the rest of us got stuck with higher prices and weaker dollars.

Now, I'll admit, leaving the gold standard wasn't *entirely* a bad move. In some ways, it did fuel economic expansion and cemented the US as a global financial powerhouse. But the problem wasn't the decision itself—it was how recklessly it was managed. If the government and both political parties had simply ensured that this newly created wealth actually benefited *all* Americans, we could have had a thriving middle class *and* an economy where the rich were still unfathomably wealthy. Instead, they funneled the money straight into the pockets of the ultrarich, fueling a wave of wealth inequality that's accelerated into a defining crisis of our time.

And now?

We're the ones paying the price.

WILL INFLATION EVER GET TO ZERO?

You'd think the government would do everything possible to eliminate inflation so our money doesn't get eaten away year after year like a slow-moving termite infestation. But the truth is, both the government *and* the wealthy benefit from inflation.

Why? Because mild inflation makes debt cheaper over time. When the value of the dollar falls, the trillions in national debt don't look quite as overwhelming. What cost the government "a dollar" decades ago may only cost them "seventy cents" today in real terms. That's why, despite speeches about "fighting inflation," there's always a quiet incentive to let it run a little hotter.

The wealthy benefit in a similar way. Inflation often drives up the value of hard assets like real estate, stocks, and commodities—things they already own in abundance. While everyday Americans watch prices at the grocery store eat away at their paychecks, the wealthy see their portfolios grow, their properties appreciate, and their debts become easier to manage. Inflation quietly shifts the balance of power further in their favor.

Take Nikki, for example. She bought a home in 2004 with a $100,000 mortgage. Her payment was about $600 a month for principal and interest—a decent chunk back then. Fast-forward to today, and she's still paying $600. But now, because of inflation, that same $600 feels small. That's how inflation erodes the value of debt. For the government and the wealthy, it's a feature. For ordinary Americans, it's a bug—one that shows up at the gas pump, the grocery aisle, and in the rising cost of simply existing.

GOVERNMENT WASTE: WHERE DOES OUR MONEY ACTUALLY GO?

Here's the most frustrating part: We already pay an enormous amount in taxes. If the government wasn't wasting and mismanaging our money, we wouldn't have to constantly borrow and print more.

But instead of fixing the root causes of our problems, they double down on bad policies and ask us to keep trusting the system.

Many government programs start with good intentions, but once they're in place, they become nearly impossible to reform no matter how inefficient they are.

Take welfare programs and Social Security. These were created to help people, and they absolutely do provide critical support for millions of Americans. The problem isn't the people who rely on them—it's that the government often runs these programs in ways that trap people in cycles of dependency instead of giving them real pathways to financial freedom.

Imagine if, instead of pouring trillions into inefficient systems, we invested more heavily in education, skills training, and real economic opportunities. Imagine if people were empowered to build wealth on their own terms, while still having a safety net for tough times. Imagine if individuals had more control over their retirement savings, instead of being forced to trust that the government will manage it responsibly. That's the kind of future that would actually lift the middle class—one where support systems exist but don't suffocate opportunity.

Right now, though? We're stuck with a system that overreaches, overspends, and leaves everyday taxpayers footing the bill. We work hard, pay 20 to 30 percent of our income in taxes, and too often feel like we're getting very little in return.

Which brings me to the biggest scam we've all accepted as normal: *taxes.*

TAXES

Let's talk about something we all feel every time payday rolls around: taxes. We've accepted them as a normal part of life, but most of us have never stopped to ask, "How did we get here?" And more importantly, "Is there a better way?"

Income tax, for example, didn't even exist until 1913, when the Sixteenth Amendment was passed. Social Security and Medicare taxes (FICA) didn't come along until 1937. Back then, they were tiny—just 1 percent each for employee and employer. Today, they're 7.65 percent each, and together with income tax, they eat up a huge share of every paycheck. We're left carrying the fallout of past administrations' choices while the value of our dollar continues to shrink.

And here's the bigger problem: This cycle doesn't stop with inflation. When that isn't enough, taxes become the go-to solution. That's why younger generations often feel like they're being squeezed from both ends—prices climbing on one side, tax burdens growing on the other.

Earlier generations, meanwhile, were able to build wealth in a system that—while never perfect—gave ordinary Americans a fighting chance. A single income could often cover a home, raise a family, and still leave room to save for retirement. Housing costs were in line with wages, higher education was affordable, and the average worker had a real shot at buying assets that grew with the economy.

That's the opportunity millennials and Gen Z are craving—not a handout but a level playing field. The difference is that decades of economic policy have tilted the game. Instead of rewarding work, stability, and savings, today's system favors debt, speculation, and asset holders. And that's why it feels so much harder to replicate the financial stability our parents and grandparents built. And while big-picture policies explain part of the struggle, the weight also shows up in our everyday lives—in the way taxes touch almost everything we do.

Taxes aren't just about money—they're about ownership and control. Every April, we're reminded of how much of our hard work gets redirected before we ever see it. But the impact goes far beyond income tax.

Think about homeownership. Even if you pay off your mortgage after decades of sacrifice, you never truly own your home. Property taxes mean you have a "forever rent" to the government. Fall behind, and the house you worked so hard for can be taken away.

The same is true for your car. Pay it off, and you'd think it's yours—but each year you still owe registration, taxes, and fees just to keep it on the road. Miss a payment? The penalties can pile up fast.

And income? The money you wake up early for, the hours you sacrifice for, the value you create—before you even touch it, the government takes their share. If you're self-employed, it can feel like an even bigger punch.

Take Jerome, who left corporate life to start his own pressure-washing business. After grinding through a tough first year, he finally pulled in $90,000—more than he ever earned before. But tax season was a wake-up call: nearly $28,000 gone. Unlike W-2 employees, Jerome had to pay both the employer and employee share of Social Security and Medicare, plus income tax. He spent countless hours tracking expenses, saving receipts, and navigating a maze of paperwork—time he could have spent building his business.

When he learned about forming an S Corp to reduce his burden, it came with even more complexity: registering with the state, filing new returns, hiring accountants. In a system that was supposed to reward hard work and innovation, Jerome felt punished for taking a risk.

And he's not alone. Millions of people experience the same

frustration. We're taxed when we earn, taxed when we save, taxed when we spend, and taxed when we own. And despite all this, we're constantly told we're "not paying our fair share."

This isn't just about dollars—it's about freedom. Right now, the government takes first claim on everything we earn, own, and build. But the less power we hand over, the more control we keep over our own lives. And while we might not be able to change the entire system overnight, we *can* educate ourselves, play the game wisely, and look for every legal way to minimize the damage.

Because at the end of the day, money is more than currency—it's time, freedom, and the future we're working toward.

SOCIAL SECURITY: A PROMISE UNDER PRESSURE

When Social Security was created in the 1930s, it was a revolutionary idea: a safety net to ensure Americans wouldn't face poverty in old age. Workers contributed a small share of their paycheck—just 1 percent at first—and when they retired, the system promised them stability. For decades, it worked well. With more than a dozen workers supporting each retiree in the 1950s, the fund had plenty of cushion.

But times have changed. Today, only about 2.5 workers support each retiree. People are living longer, birth rates have declined, and the math no longer works the way it once did. By 2033, the Social Security trust fund is projected to run dry, which could mean a 21 percent cut in benefits unless something changes.

Here's the catch: The money we contribute through payroll taxes doesn't sit in a personal account earning interest. Instead, today's workers are paying today's retirees. That system worked in the past, but for millennials and Gen Z, it creates a different reality. We're paying more in, but our odds of seeing the same level of benefit are slim.

And here's an important detail most people don't realize: Social Security and Medicare are funded through *payroll taxes*. Each paycheck, employees see 7.65 percent taken out under the label "FICA." But that's only half the story—employers match that amount, meaning the true cost is 15.3 percent. For traditional workers, you don't "see" the employer side, but if you're self-employed or an independent contractor (a growing reality today with gig work and side hustles), you're on the hook for both halves. That means 15.3 percent of your income goes straight to the government before you ever think about income tax, rent, or groceries. For many freelancers, that's a huge weight that makes saving and investing even harder.

Take Riley, twenty-three, earning $40,000 a year. Right out of college, Riley is contributing 7.65 percent of every paycheck to Social Security and Medicare—that's about $3,060 a year. For many young workers at this income level, that payroll tax is actually *more than their effective federal income tax rate* once deductions and credits are applied. In other words, Riley is paying more to a system that may not fully deliver than to the IRS itself.

Over a lifetime of work, Riley will contribute roughly $380,000 into Social Security. And yes, benefits do come with a cost-of-living adjustment (COLA), so the monthly check will likely be higher in the future than today's average of $1,900. But here's the catch: COLAs are designed to *keep up with inflation, not to build wealth*. That means Riley's future payments will only maintain purchasing power—not grow it. In fact, when you factor in rising costs of housing, health care, and everyday living, Riley could still end up with less real value than what they contributed.

Even if Riley collects benefits for twenty-five years, the total payout often ends up far less than what they put in—especially compared to what that same money could have grown into in a Roth IRA or index fund over four decades of compounding. And unlike those investments, Social Security contributions can't freely be passed down to children or grandchildren. Yes, there are survivor benefits: A spouse may be eligible to receive payments (though often losing their own Social Security in the process), and dependent children who are minors, disabled, or still in school may qualify. But once those conditions end, the benefits stop. For most families, the contributions simply vanish back into the system.

When Social Security was first introduced, the system made more sense. Housing was affordable, the cost of living was lower, and wages stretched further. Families could cover their needs on a single income, and the promise of a government safety net felt both reassuring and realistic. Back then, there were also far more workers supporting each retiree, so the math worked out.

But fast-forward to today, and the landscape looks completely different. With only about 2.5 workers per retiree, skyrocketing housing costs, and wages that haven't kept pace with inflation, the system is under immense strain. What once felt like a solid promise now feels shaky for younger generations. The hope that Social Security once represented has been replaced with uncertainty about whether the system can keep up—or whether our contributions will ever come back to us in full.

That's why many younger Americans feel like they're being asked to prop up a system that may never fully deliver for them. The goalposts keep moving—full retirement age has already shifted from sixty-five to nearly sixty-seven, and it may rise further. Unless we live to one hundred, many of us may never see the full benefits we're paying for.

This doesn't mean Social Security should disappear—it means it needs reform. A system designed for a different era can't simply be patched forever. Without changes, younger generations inherit not only the cost but also the uncertainty of a program that no longer matches modern reality.

Social Security was built as a promise. To keep that promise alive, it needs to be rebuilt for a new era. Here are a few suggestions that we could consider.

1. REMOVE THE $176,100 CAP—TAX EVERYONE FAIRLY

Right now, only income up to $176,100 is subject to Social Security tax. That means a billionaire pays the same Social Security tax as someone making $176,100 a year. If we simply taxed all income at the same 6.2 percent rate, the system would be far better funded and more sustainable for future generations.

2. PHASE OUT SOCIAL SECURITY FOR MILLENNIALS AND GEN Z—GIVE US THE OPTION TO OPT OUT

Let's be honest—most younger Americans don't believe Social Security will be there for them anyway. So why not offer an opt-out option?

- Gen X and boomers would still receive the benefits they were promised.
- Millennials and Gen Zers could choose to keep their 6.2 percent and invest it in the stock market over the next thirty-plus years. Historically, even modest investments in index funds would yield far higher returns than Social Security ever could.

3. PAIR THESE POLICIES WITH FINANCIAL EDUCATION AND A NARRATIVE SHIFT

Fixing Social Security isn't just about policy—it's also about education and mindset.

- Financial literacy should be mandatory in high schools so that young people understand how to invest and build wealth outside of government programs.
- Politicians and the media need to shift the conversation from dependency on Social Security to wealth building through assets like stocks, real estate, and retirement accounts.

LOOKING AHEAD: BEYOND SOCIAL SECURITY

Even with reforms, there's a deeper question we'll have to face. Social Security was built on the assumption that most Americans would spend forty years in traditional jobs, steadily contributing payroll taxes. But the economy is changing fast. Automation, AI, and shifting labor markets could dramatically reduce the number of stable, full-time jobs in the future. If fewer people are working the kinds of jobs that fund Social Security, the system will struggle no matter how we tweak it.

That's why some economists and policymakers are already discussing bigger ideas—like universal basic income (UBI). Instead of relying on payroll taxes, UBI would guarantee every citizen a base level of income funded by broader sources such as corporate taxes, wealth taxes, or even dividends from emerging technologies. The idea is simple: If machines and algorithms do more of the work, the gains should flow back to society, not just to shareholders.

UBI may sound radical, but so did Social Security in the 1930s. At its core, both are about ensuring dignity and stability when markets alone fall short. Whether the future holds reforms to Social Security, a shift toward UBI, or some hybrid model, one thing is certain: The systems that worked for past generations won't automatically work for ours.

And that's the bigger theme we're stepping into next—how late-stage capitalism has reshaped not just retirement but every corner of the economy.

Chapter 7

LATE-STAGE CAPITALISM

Capitalism. Socialism. Democratic socialism. Communism.

We hear these "isms" thrown around constantly, especially by younger generations who are increasingly frustrated with the system we live under: capitalism. But why? On one hand, capitalism is the engine that built the largest economy in world history. It helped America rise to the top, driving breakthroughs in technology, healthcare, and industry. At its best, it created the strongest middle class the world had ever seen. For decades, an average worker with a decent job could buy a home, raise a family, and retire with dignity. That was capitalism working more smoothly—when growth and opportunity were more widely shared.

But over the last fifty years, small tweaks—tax cuts, deregulation, financial engineering—have contorted that system. What was once a powerful wealth-building engine for the many has shifted into a system that primarily serves corporations and the wealthy few. Yes, we still call it capitalism, but unchecked, it's morphed into what many now describe as late-stage capitalism—a version where profits are extracted at the expense of workers, families, and communities.

Before we dive into what late-stage capitalism looks like today, it's worth taking a quick pause to define these "isms" that dominate so much of the conversation:

- **Capitalism:** an economic system where private individuals and companies own the means of production—businesses, land, resources—and operate them for profit.
- **Socialism:** a system where the government (or society collectively) owns or heavily regulates key industries and resources, aiming to distribute wealth more evenly.
- **Democratic socialism:** a hybrid approach—capitalism exists, but with stronger safety nets, regulations, and public services to reduce inequality (think free college or universal healthcare layered on top of a market economy).
- **Communism:** in theory, a classless, stateless society where all property is publicly owned and wealth is shared equally. In practice, historical attempts often concentrated power in the hands of the state.

Most Americans don't want pure socialism or communism. What they want is fairness—a system where hard work can once again buy stability and opportunity. That's why younger generations are so disillusioned. They see the promise of capitalism but also the ways it's been distorted.

So, what did capitalism look like when it worked more smoothly—before big box, private equity, and policy changes twisted it?

Back in the twentieth century, the American Dream for small business often looked like this: Someone with a skill or an idea—let's call him Henry—saved diligently until he had enough to open a shop. Maybe it was a hardware store, a diner, a fabric shop. He hired locally, reinvested profits into the business, and helped create stability for his family and his town. One person's hard work sparked a ripple effect: New businesses opened nearby, neighbors had steady paychecks, and the community thrived.

Henry isn't a real person, but he is a stand-in for the thousands of mom-and-pop shops that once dotted America's towns. But if you grew up in a town like mine, Ashtabula, Ohio, you know this story because you lived it.

When I was a kid, Ashtabula was a proud working-class city. We had steel plants, factories, a bustling harbor, and even a thriving mall when I was in high school. Families shopped locally. People had stable jobs. And the town felt alive. But then Walmart opened in 1995, right next to the mall. At first, it felt like progress: low prices, one-stop convenience. But like in so many communities, Walmart became the tipping point. Foot traffic drained from the mall; anchor stores began to close; and small local shops couldn't keep up.

My grandfather owned a craft store—something like a smaller Jo-Ann Fabrics—and for years it was a community staple. Over time, though, crafting slowed down, and when Walmart moved in, it was a nail in the coffin. My grandfather's store eventually closed, and with it went another piece of Ashtabula's identity.

Around the same time, the once-booming Ashtabula Mall began to fade. Back in the day, it had everything—a movie theater, restaurants, a buzzing food court, an arcade, and anchor stores like Dillard's, JCPenney, and Kmart lining the halls. It was alive, energetic, and central to our town's social life. But slowly, like so many malls across America, the rise of Walmart and later Amazon absorbed its lifeblood. Now when I visit, the mall feels like a ghost town. Only a handful of stores remain, and walking through what was once my stomping ground with friends is like stepping into a hollow shell of memories.

What happened in Ashtabula wasn't unique. Across America, studies found that Walmart often replaced better-paying retail jobs with lower-wage, less secure ones. Instead of adding economic value, it reshuffled it—draining life from Main Streets and malls and consolidating wealth and power at the top. The story wasn't just about one company's low prices; it was about how corporate consolidation slowly hollowed out local economies.

Fast-forward to 2025, and the landscape looks even harsher under late-stage capitalism. Jobs are less secure. Workers are pushed into freelancing and gig work without benefits. And the balance of power inside corporations has tilted beyond recognition. A few decades ago, CEOs earned around ten times what their workers made. Today, it's not uncommon for CEOs to earn hundreds of times more, while employees live in fear of being downsized.

And it's not just big-box stores hollowing out communities. Enter private equity. Firms with billions in capital buy up local businesses, load them with debt, cut costs, and flip them for a payday. They don't care about the product, the employees, or the town. They care about turning investments into profits within a short period of time. Even if that means layoffs, higher prices, and worse service. The businesses that once supported a community become nothing more than line items on a balance sheet.

This isn't just theory. As Brendan Ballou, former federal prosecutor and author of "Private Equity Is Gutting America—and Getting Away with It," explained in a guest essay in *The New York Times*:

> *Companies bought by private equity firms are far more likely to go bankrupt than companies that aren't. Over the last decade, private equity firms were responsible for nearly 600,000 job losses in the retail sector alone. In nursing homes, where the firms have been particularly active, private equity ownership is responsible for an estimated—and astounding—20,000 premature deaths over a 12-year period, according to a recent working paper from the National Bureau of Economic Research. Similar tales of woe abound in mobile homes, prison health care, emergency medicine, ambulances, apartment buildings, and elsewhere. Yet private equity and its leaders continue to prosper, and executives of the top firms are billionaires many times over.*[58]

This is the shift from capitalism at its best to capitalism at its worst. Once, hard work and risk-taking could build something lasting, lifting up both families and communities. Today, unchecked consolidation and private equity have warped that promise. To understand what's happening, we need to look closer at the players fueling this transformation: asset managers, private equity firms, and hedge funds.

ASSET MANAGERS: THE GIANTS THAT OWN EVERYTHING

Asset management firms oversee investments for individuals, corporations, and even governments. Their job is to grow and manage wealth by investing in things like stocks, bonds, real estate, and even entire industries.

BlackRock is the largest asset manager in the world, overseeing roughly $12.5 trillion in assets as of 2025. That single firm manages more capital than the annual economic output of nearly every country on the planet—except the United States and China—a reminder of just how concentrated financial power has become.[59]

Rather than buying homes directly, asset managers like BlackRock invest through REITs and publicly traded companies that own and operate large portfolios of single-family homes. Another major player is Vanguard, which holds significant stakes in homebuilders, real estate firms, and rental companies. They don't own homes outright, but their capital helps shape who can compete for them.

Here's how the system works. Asset managers don't decide which industries should dominate the economy; their index funds are designed to follow performance. When housing becomes scarce and rents rise, companies that own large numbers of homes perform well. As those companies grow, they enter major indexes—and trillions of dollars in passive investment automatically flow toward them. That capital lowers their cost of capital, allowing large housing operators to scale faster than individual buyers ever could. The result isn't a conspiracy—it's a feedback loop. Scarcity makes housing profitable, profitability attracts capital, and capital accelerates consolidation.

This isn't an argument for eliminating asset managers or ending capitalism. It's an argument for updating the rules of a system that was never designed for capital at this scale. Because when ownership concentrates and participation shrinks, we don't get a healthier market—we get a Monopoly board where one side accumulates ownership while everyone else funds the game.

Every system needs speed limits. When capital can move faster than wages, savings, or families can respond, the outcome is predictable: concentration at the top and erosion everywhere else. That doesn't mean stopping capital—it means slowing it where it overwhelms basic participation. One example would be placing sensible limits on how much institutional capital can concentrate in sectors tied to essential needs, like housing—not to punish success, but to prevent scale from quietly hollowing out the middle class.

PRIVATE EQUITY FIRMS: THE HOUSE FLIPPERS ON STEROIDS

If asset managers influence markets indirectly, private equity firms operate much more hands-on. Understanding the difference matters—because while these firms often get lumped together, they play very different roles in the economy.

Private equity firms pool money from wealthy investors and institutions to buy assets outright, take control of them, restructure their operations, and eventually sell them for profit. Unlike asset managers, who largely track markets, private equity firms actively shape outcomes. They don't just influence prices—they decide strategy, staffing, pricing, and long-term direction.

To be clear, private equity isn't inherently bad. At its best, it can rescue struggling companies, improve efficiency, and provide capital where traditional lenders won't. Many businesses—and jobs—have survived because private equity stepped in when no one else would.

But that same model can become deeply disruptive when applied to essential goods like housing or when financial efficiency is optimized at the expense of long-term resilience.

One of the most influential players in this space is Blackstone (not to be confused with BlackRock). In the aftermath of the 2008 housing crash, Blackstone began purchasing tens of thousands of foreclosed single-family homes across the United States, particularly in hard-hit Sunbelt markets. Rather than selling those homes back into the market, they were consolidated into a massive rental operation.[60]

Over time, that portfolio became one of the largest single-family rental platforms in the country, eventually spun off as a public company. Blackstone later exited its position after generating billions in profits—but for many families, the opportunity to buy back into homeownership never returned. Rents rose, supply tightened, and ownership shifted permanently away from households and toward institutional landlords.

This wasn't passive investing or an unintended side effect. It was a deliberate strategy and one that worked exactly as designed. Buy distressed assets cheaply, convert them into long-term income streams, and extract value from scarcity.

Private equity can play a productive role in the economy, but when leverage and short time horizons collide with essential goods, guardrails are needed.

HEDGE FUNDS: THE SPECULATORS BETTING ON YOUR RENT

If asset managers influence markets through scale, and private equity reshapes them through control, hedge funds operate on speed. Their goal isn't to own something forever or patiently build it over time. It's to move fast, take risks, and profit from short-term market shifts. Pure hedge funds don't usually buy homes directly. Instead, they interact with housing through financial markets—trading mortgage-backed securities, housing-linked bonds, REITs, and derivatives tied to home prices, interest rates, and credit conditions.

Firms like Citadel and Bridgewater Associates don't manage rental homes or operate housing companies. They trade around housing—betting on how fast prices move, how interest rates shift, and how credit conditions change. In this world, housing isn't a place to live; it's a financial signal.

Those trades don't stay on Wall Street. When large pools of fast-moving capital pour into housing-linked markets, they can influence mortgage rates, amplify price swings, and increase volatility—effects that ripple outward to renters and buyers who never chose to be part of the trade.

Hedge funds are not inherently reckless, nor are they solely responsible for past crises. But when high-speed, high-leverage strategies collide with essential goods like housing, the consequences can spread far beyond financial markets. Basic living costs become tied to market dynamics households have no control over.

This isn't a story of bad actors. It's about mismatch. Housing moves slowly. Financial markets move fast. And when something people need to survive gets pulled into high-speed trading systems, stability takes a back seat. The faster the game moves, the harder it becomes for regular people to keep up.

HOW THIS IMPACTS YOU

All of this financial machinery shows up in everyday life in simple ways: higher prices, fewer choices, and rising rents.

In many markets, first-time buyers aren't just competing with other families—they're competing with institutional investors who can move faster, pay in bulk, and absorb losses individuals can't. Homes that once would have gone to owners are increasingly funneled into long-term rental pools.

The shift has been rapid. Over the past decade, Wall Street–backed investors have accumulated hundreds of thousands of single-family homes, with the heaviest concentration in fast-growing Sunbelt states like Georgia, Arizona, Texas, and Florida. In some of these markets, institutional buyers now make up a significant share of rental housing and new investor purchases.

And the trend extends beyond houses. Large investment firms have expanded their ownership of apartment buildings and mobile home parks—sectors that once offered relatively affordable housing—often followed by rent increases and new fees that strain already-tight household budgets.

The result is a quiet but profound change. Families who might have owned homes a generation ago are increasingly locked into renting, while ownership concentrates in fewer hands. Much of this consolidation happens out of sight, through complex financial structures that obscure who ultimately controls the housing—until the consequences show up in monthly payments.

HOW REITS QUIETLY RESHAPE COMMUNITIES

To understand how Wall Street enters housing at scale, you have to look at REITs—real estate investment trusts. A REIT is a company that pools money from investors—including pension funds, institutions, and asset managers—and uses that capital to buy real estate. Think of it like a mutual fund for property: instead of investing in stocks, you're investing in apartments, rental homes, or even mobile home parks.

Here's where it gets a bit complicated. When large REITs acquire homes, they don't show up in town under a single recognizable corporate name. Properties are typically held through layers of LLCs, small, local-sounding entities created for liability protection and financing purposes. On paper, it can look like many separate landlords are buying homes. In reality, those LLCs often roll up to the same large corporate owner or REIT backed by institutional capital.

Regardless of the structure, the effect on local markets is the same: concentrated buying power that regular families can't compete with. This structure also fragments accountability. When tenants face rent hikes, added fees, or poor maintenance, their listed landlord may be a shell LLC with little public information. Tracing ownership often leads back through multiple layers before reaching the corporate parent.

The end result is subtle but powerful. Large landlords can steadily build massive portfolios across communities without attracting much attention, until rents rise, housing becomes scarce, and the market feels increasingly out of reach for everyday families.

HOW DID WE GET HERE? THE POLICY CHANGES THAT OPENED THE DOOR FOR WALL STREET

If you want to understand why buying a home feels impossible today, you have to look at the last two decades of policy decisions. Each one, often with good intentions on paper, ended up tilting the housing market further in Wall Street's favor.

1. THE 2008 HOUSING CRASH: WALL STREET'S PERFECT OPPORTUNITY

The housing crisis wasn't just a disaster—it was a gold mine for Wall Street.

Before 2008, banks handed out risky mortgages to people who couldn't afford them. When the bubble burst, millions of Americans lost their homes to foreclosure. But while families were packing up their lives, Wall Street was gearing up for the biggest housing clearance sale in modern history.

Instead of regular families scooping up foreclosures, private equity firms and institutional investors swooped in and bought thousands of homes for pennies on the dollar. The government even encouraged this, desperate to stabilize the market. Programs were created to move distressed properties in bulk, and policymakers hoped institutional buyers would help absorb excess supply and prevent further price collapse.

Key Policy Change: The Federal Reserve slashed interest rates to near zero, making it easier for big firms to borrow money and buy homes in bulk—while regular Americans were still reeling from job losses and ruined credit.

The result? Instead of homeowners, we got landlords. For families, it was the loss of the American Dream. For Wall Street, it was buy-one-get-one-free housing.

This was the moment housing shifted: no longer just a home for families, but an investment vehicle for financial giants.

2. THE RISE OF REITS AND "FINANCIALIZED" HOUSING

By the 1980s and 1990s, policy shifts allowed REITs to explode in popularity. Think of them as mutual funds, but for real estate: investors pool money, and the REIT buys properties. That meant housing was no longer just shelter. It became an asset class, something to be traded on Wall Street like a stock. By the 2010s, massive companies like Invitation Homes (backed by Blackstone) were buying tens of thousands of single-family homes, turning them into long-term rental machines.[61]

Key Policy Change: Favorable tax laws gave institutional landlords incentives to buy and hold, making it more profitable to rent out homes than to sell them to families.

The result? Homes that once would've gone to first-time buyers became permanent rental stock owned by corporations. For Wall Street, it was passive income. For families, it was another door slammed shut.

And now, Wall Street wasn't just a player in housing—it was beginning to dominate it.

3. QE AND CHEAP MONEY FLOODING THE MARKET

In the previous chapter, we talked about the Fed "printing money." That's quantitative easing (QE)—a policy where the Federal Reserve creates money to buy financial assets, including mortgage-backed securities. The goal was to jumpstart the economy after the crash (and again during COVID-19). But the side effect was devastating for aspiring homeowners.

Key Policy Change: QE made money cheap to borrow, but not everyone had the same access to low-cost credit. Large institutions could borrow easily and scale into housing, while everyday buyers faced higher prices and tougher mortgage approvals.[62]

The result? Wall Street used the cheap money to outbid families, driving home prices even higher. The same policy meant to help Main Street ended up turbocharging Wall Street's housing empire.

Each round of QE widened the gap: Investors got richer, families got priced out.

4. THE 2017 TAX CUTS AND JOBS ACT (TCJA): A BOON FOR INVESTORS

In 2017, the Tax Cuts and Jobs Act delivered significant new advantages to corporations and real estate investors. Corporate tax rates were slashed, and property owners gained additional benefits—most notably a 20 percent pass-through deduction for many real estate businesses and expanded depreciation rules that allowed investors to write off certain improvements much faster.

These changes made it more profitable to buy, hold, and rent out properties rather than sell them. The tax code increasingly rewarded long-term ownership and rental income—tilting incentives away from putting homes back on the market for families.

Key Policy Change: Investors could deduct a larger share of income and expenses, lowering their effective tax rates and strengthening the financial case for accumulating rental portfolios.

The result was further pressure on supply. Families searching for homes faced fewer options, while institutional landlords benefited from policies that encouraged holding assets instead of turning them over. A tax law marketed as pro-growth ended up reinforcing dynamics that made homeownership harder to reach for many Americans.

5. COVID-19 AND THE REAL ESTATE FRENZY

The pandemic poured gasoline on the fire.

With trillions in stimulus money, rock-bottom interest rates, and eviction moratoriums, Wall Street saw housing as the safest bet around—and investors went all in.

Key Policy Change: The Fed kept interest rates near zero for too long, giving institutional buyers access to cheap capital just as demand for housing was exploding.

The result was twofold:

- **Housing turned into a frenzy.** Institutional buyers had two huge advantages: ultralow borrowing costs and the ability to make lightning-fast, all-cash offers that regular buyers couldn't match.
- **More renters, fewer owners.** Families who hadn't bought before the summer of 2022 were increasingly priced out, forced to remain renters while corporate landlords expanded their reach.

In the middle of a pandemic—when people most needed stability—housing became the hottest investment on Wall Street's menu.

Investors made a fortune. Families who dreamed of owning a home were left behind.

FROM HOUSING TO BUSINESSES: THE PRIVATE EQUITY PLAYBOOK

Private equity started moving heavily into housing after the 2008 financial crisis, when foreclosures gave firms like Blackstone a golden opportunity to scoop up thousands of homes at bargain prices. But housing wasn't their first rodeo.

Private equity originally made its name in the world of business acquisitions. The model was simple: Raise money from investors, buy struggling companies, and try to improve them. In the best-case scenario, the firm would modernize operations, expand into new markets, and eventually sell the business for a profit. Sometimes, this approach really does work—and not every PE deal is a doomsday story.

But there's a darker side. Over the decades, private equity shifted from "building businesses" to "financial engineering." The key weapon? *Leveraged buyouts (LBOs).*

Here's how it works: Instead of buying a company with their own money, PE firms borrow massive amounts of debt to finance the purchase—then stick that debt on the company they just bought. Suddenly, a once-stable business is saddled with billions in interest payments it never had before. That money doesn't go into better products or paying workers—it goes to paying off loans and enriching investors.

And to make things even sweeter for themselves, private equity executives benefit from a tax loophole called *carried interest*.

Let's look at an example using round numbers. Imagine Caroline runs a private equity firm. She raises $1 billion from investors—pension funds, university endowments, wealthy families. Her team puts in a tiny amount of their own money (maybe 1 percent at most). Then they use that $1 billion to buy a company.

Fast-forward seven years. They sell the company, and it's now worth $2 billion. The investors get back their $1 billion plus most of the profits. But Caroline and her team take 20 percent of the gains as their fee for managing the deal. In this case, that's $200 million. Now here's the trick:

Most of us would assume Caroline's $200 million is *income*—basically a performance bonus for running the deal.

But private equity firms convinced Washington that this should count as *capital gains*, not salary.

Capital gains are taxed at a much lower rate than income. So instead of paying the top tax rate of 37 percent like a doctor or lawyer would on a big paycheck, Caroline pays closer to 20 percent.

Critics argue this is outrageous because Caroline wasn't really risking her own money. She was managing other people's money and taking a cut of the upside. In plain English: It's a management fee dressed up as an investment.

Defenders of the loophole say: "Well, Caroline only gets paid if the investment is successful, so she is taking on risk." But let's be real—she didn't risk $1 billion of her own cash. She risked someone else's money, then collected a bonus when it worked out.

This is why the *carried interest loophole* has been in politicians' agenda for years. Presidents from both parties have promised to close it. Yet somehow, every time reform comes up, lobbyists swoop in and the loophole survives.

This is where things start to break down. While some firms genuinely improve the businesses they buy, others bleed them dry—through debt, fees, and asset stripping—until bankruptcy is almost inevitable. And when the collapse comes, it's workers, communities, and customers who pay the price.

HOW PRIVATE EQUITY KILLED A GIANT: THE TOYS "R" US STORY

Like I mentioned, there are many private equity deals that do help businesses as intended, but others get completely devastated.

I recently sat down with Tiffany Cianci on *The Freddie Smith Podcast*, and she gave me a master class on the brutal realities of private equity. She detailed the heart-wrenching demise of Toys "R" Us at the hands of private equity. For many of us, Toys "R" Us wasn't just a store, it was a core memory of our childhoods. The excitement of walking through those aisles, the joy of picking out a toy, and Geoffrey the Giraffe.

If you grew up in the '80s or '90s, you probably remember that jingle: "I don't wanna grow up, I'm a Toys 'R' Us kid . . ." It was the Disneyland of toy stores. It was magic. They weren't just selling toys; they were selling childhood memories. But behind the shelves of Barbies and Nintendos, a slow-moving financial heist was underway. And it was all legal.

In 2005, three private equity firms—Bain Capital, KKR, and Vornado Realty Trust—bought Toys "R" Us in what's known as a leveraged buyout (LBO) for $6.6 billion. But they didn't actually *have* $6.6 billion. No, that would require actual skin in the game. Instead, they borrowed more than $5.3 billion of it, and here's the catch: They made Toys "R" Us borrow the money.[63] The very company being bought was forced to carry the weight of its own purchase.

Before this takeover, Toys "R" Us was profitable and relatively stable. Afterward, they were drowning in debt. They now owed nearly half a billion dollars a year in interest payments alone. That's $400–$500 million annually, money that no longer went to improving stores, competing with Amazon, or creating a better customer experience. It just disappeared into a financial black hole.

And it gets worse.

Private equity firms weren't content just bleeding the company dry with debt. They charged massive "advisory" fees, millions every year, for services like operations, finance, and management, often signing contracts with themselves on both ends. Then they sold the land under Toys "R" Us stores to their own real estate investment trusts, forcing the company to lease it back at jacked-up prices. They sold off the warehouses. The trucking fleet. Even the emergency inventory that helped them ride out slow quarters—all gone.

Every asset that gave Toys "R" Us the foundation to survive was stripped away and sold. Dividends were funneled back to the private equity firms. And when the business could no longer keep up with the artificial debt load, it collapsed. *More than thirty thousand employees lost their jobs.* Not because the store wasn't loved. Not because it couldn't compete. But because it was gutted from the inside out.

This wasn't a failed business plan. It was a business model that succeeded, just not for the company. For the private equity firms, it worked beautifully.

They got their money out early. They took their profits. And when the company went bankrupt, they walked away with clean hands, because they were never the ones on the hook for the debt.

Toys "R" Us may feel like a story from the past, but it was really just a warning shot. And it's not stopping with toys or even housing. Private equity has been quietly moving into almost every corner of our daily lives. Daycares. Assisted-living centers. Veterinary clinics. Dentist offices. Even the pest control guy who shows up at your door.

You think you're choosing a mom-and-pop business. In reality? You're choosing Wall Street. It's the illusion of choice. Just like when you walk into a grocery store and see a hundred brands on the shelf—but behind them are the same ten corporations pulling the strings.

That's the playbook. Strip down the business, jack up the prices, and funnel the profits to investors who may not even live in this country. And if we don't put guardrails on private equity, we're heading toward a future where every essential service we depend on—from our housing, to our healthcare, to grandma's nursing home—is owned and operated by the same handful of financial giants.

The American Dream wasn't supposed to look like this. But if we're not paying attention, it's exactly where we're headed.

Chapter 8

WEALTH INEQUALITY

Any time we bring up the wealth gap or talk about how the sys-tem feels fixed against us, someone inevitably chimes in: "You're just jealous of the rich."

We're not. We're just fed up with getting continually fucked.

For a long time, we actually *loved* rich people. Millennials grew up idolizing wealth. We were glued to *MTV Cribs*, *Lifestyles of the Rich and Famous*, *Keeping Up with the Kardashians*, *The Real Housewives*. Even when celebrities and rich influencers started posting on Instagram, we were fascinated. Seeing someone post from Mykonos while we were eating ramen in our $800-a-month apartment wasn't upsetting. It was entertaining. Because back then, we still had something important: *hope*.

Starter homes under $200K. Rent that didn't eat up half a paycheck. A little savings. A weekend road trip to look forward to. Life was manageable. You didn't have to be rich to feel okay.

That feeling is gone.

Now, when we see billionaires flying to space or influencers casually unboxing $50,000 handbags, it doesn't feel aspirational anymore, it feels like a slap in the face. Because while they were floating away on yachts, we were watching rent double, groceries skyrocket, student loans pile up, and dreams slip further out of reach.

Here's the visual I keep coming back to: Imagine the wealthy as a giant hot air balloon. For decades, the middle class was the basket tied below by ropes. As the balloon rose, we rose too. The rich got richer, but we didn't mind—because our lives were rising right along with theirs.

But over the last fifty years, one by one, those ropes were cut. Wages stopped keeping up with productivity. Housing prices exploded. Healthcare costs ballooned. Education became unaffordable. And then, during the pandemic, the last rope snapped.

The balloon soared into the sky.

The basket?

It started to fall.

And without those ropes, it makes it extremely difficult to climb up anymore.

Back in the 1970s, a unionized grocery store worker making four dollars an hour could put in forty hours a week, buy a home, raise a family, and retire with a pension.

Today, you can work fifty hours a week, have a degree, a side hustle, a savings strategy, and a spreadsheet tracking every dollar—and still not comfortably afford rent without a roommate. Sure, some people manage to pull it off, but it's harder than ever.

Today, you've got to be extraordinary just to live an ordinary life.

We just want what Americans had for decades: wages that rise with productivity, housing that's within reach, and the ability to work a full-time job and build a decent life.

If the gap keeps growing, it starts to look less like America—and more like the plot of a dystopian movie. Because today, the divide between the "have-yachts" and the "have-nots" has never felt wider.

THE HAVE-YACHTS AND THE HAVE-NOTS

We are eerily close to becoming a two-class society—one where the ultrarich live in a separate, untouchable world, and everyone else is left scrambling just to get by.

That dystopia might not be so far away. A United States where the wealthy live in their own isolated cities, protected by gates, private security, and drones, while the rest of us are stuck fighting for scraps in the streets.

In the 2013 movie *Elysium*, Matt Damon's character lives on a polluted, overpopulated Earth, while the rich literally live in a floating paradise in the sky, untouched by disease, poverty, or struggle. The ultrawealthy have access to instant medical care, infinite resources, and absolute security, while the rest of society is left behind to survive in filth.

When I first watched it, I thought, *Damn, what a terrifying vision of the future.*

Now it doesn't feel so far-fetched. The ultrarich aren't floating in space just yet, but they might as well be. They live in gated estates, perched up in the hills, or tucked away on private islands, completely detached from the reality the rest of us are living in. Their neighborhoods have 24/7 patrol cars, ensuring they never have to interact with the "regular" world.

They don't go to the same grocery stores, the same banks, or the same hospitals as we do. When was the last time you saw a billionaire waiting in line at CVS? You won't, because they have concierge doctors who make house calls. Need to fly somewhere? They don't sit in airport terminals, taking off their shoes at TSA like the rest of us—they fly private. Even dinner looks different for them: no waiting for a table, no Saturday night crowds, just private dining rooms or personal chefs.

Their entire existence is insulated from the struggles of normal people.

Now, are we really headed toward a sci-fi apocalypse where the wealthy live in floating cities and the rest of us fight in the dirt? I hope not. But we don't need to go that far for things to feel dystopian. Even without spaceships, the walls and barriers—literal and figurative—are already up. Private communities, private healthcare, private security, private schools. And with AI and robotics replacing more of the jobs everyday people once relied on, the distance between those two worlds could grow even wider.

So, yeah, we may not all be living in the dirt or standing in bread lines, but let's not pretend this country isn't drowning in unnecessary suffering—poverty, crime, and sickness.

When the middle class disappears, so does the American Dream. We've already normalized working seventy-hour weeks just to afford a shared apartment well into our thirties.

And if we keep heading in this direction, Gen Alpha—the kids growing up today—might be the first generation to view homeownership the way millennials view yachts and private jets: as something reserved only for the rich.

But here's the scariest part: If the gap between the ultrawealthy and everyone else keeps widening, we could reach a point where there's no such thing as upward mobility. Where no amount of hard work is enough to break through. A lot of young people under forty already feel this. Where the middle class is nothing but a memory.

I don't want to wake up fifty years from now and explain to my grandkids that there was once a time in America when:

- The average person could buy a home.
- You only had to work forty hours a week to live comfortably.
- A single income was enough to raise a family.

I don't want to sit them down and say, "There was a time when we all had a shot at a decent life—but we let it slip away."

Because once a society crosses that line—when only the wealthy can live comfortably and everyone else is stuck treading water—it rarely finds its way back. When the balance breaks, frustration builds. And eventually, people lose faith in the system altogether.

This isn't about attacking the rich, it's about protecting balance. A healthy economy depends on opportunity, not luck. If we don't close this gap, the middle class doesn't just shrink—it disappears. And when that happens, so does the American Dream.

You don't have to take my word for it. The numbers tell the story: Generational wealth inequality has exploded, fueled by decades of policies that quietly transferred opportunity upward—until what used to be basic stability became a privilege.

THE REAL TRUTH ABOUT INCOME INEQUALITY

If you've ever watched a Bernie Sanders clip online, you've probably heard him talk about wealth inequality. It doesn't matter what the context is—Bernie could be grabbing ice cream on a Saturday afternoon, and if a reporter asked what flavor he picked, he'd probably reply, "Because of the wealth of the top one percent, I am forced to get vanilla. While billionaires like Elon Musk and Jeff Bezos enjoy all the flavors, the rest of us are left with just vanilla."

It's a funny image, but the reality is far from amusing. We often hear statistics about how the top 1 percent owns ten times more wealth than the bottom 50 percent. That means 3.4 million people hold more than ten times more wealth than 170 million people combined. Those numbers are shocking, but they still don't fully capture how uneven the system has become.

So let's break it down.

Back in the late 1980s, adjusted for inflation, Americans had a combined total wealth of around $50 trillion. Today, that number has skyrocketed to over $180 trillion. If America were a corporation, the chart would say, "Wow! What growth!" This is exactly what politicians and economists promised us when they sold the idea of trickle-down economics.

But did that wealth actually trickle down?

Of the $130 trillion in new wealth created since the late 1980s, how much made its way to the bottom 50 percent of Americans—a group of 170 million people?

Just $2 trillion.

Yes, you read that right. Out of $130 trillion in newly generated wealth, only $2 trillion reached half the country. The remaining $128 trillion went to the top half. And not only did the bottom 50 percent barely see any of that new wealth, but there are now sixty million more people in that group than there were in 1989. So that extra $2 trillion was stretched across a much larger population.

Meanwhile, the top 10 percent of Americans—a group of just thirty-five million people—now hold around $119 trillion in wealth. Compare that to the bottom 50 percent, who collectively hold just about $4–$5 trillion.

So again, I ask—how exactly did trickle-down economics work?

Wealth Breakdown in America

Group	Population	Total Wealth	Percent of Nation's Wealth
Top 1 percent	3.4 million	$52 trillion	29.5 percent
Next 9 percent	30 million	$67 trillion	37 percent
Next 40 percent	136 million	$57 trillion	31 percent
Bottom 50 percent	170 million	$4.5 trillion	2.5 percent

THE MISSING MIDDLE

To really understand where the money went, we need to look at the missing middle class—the group that isn't ultrarich but also isn't struggling at the very bottom. These are the Americans who built careers when the economy still allowed them to accumulate wealth: factory workers, nurses, construction workers, police officers, grocery store managers. Many were able to buy homes before prices skyrocketed, which is where much of their $57 trillion in wealth comes from.

But what happens when millennials and Gen Z—who face record housing costs—replace this group?

If the biggest reason today's middle class accumulated wealth was through homeownership, and younger generations are priced out of the housing market, then the wealth gap won't just persist. It will widen dramatically in the decades ahead.

THE TRUTH ABOUT THE TOP 50 PERCENT

We often hear about the "top 50 percent" of Americans as if they're living a life of yachts and private jets. The truth is far less glamorous. Most of these households aren't billionaires—they're retirees, boomers, and Gen Xers, even some millennials, who bought into the system before the rules changed.

To be in the top half of wealth in America today, you need a net worth of around $193,000—much of it held in home equity and retirement accounts.[64]

Someone who entered a skilled, middle-class profession in the 1970s or 1980s could build that kind of security by doing something meaningful: working a steady job, contributing to their community, and following the path laid out in front of them. They worked full time, provided a real service, raised a family, and had space to live their life outside of work. The system rewarded that stability with affordable housing, rising wages, and assets that grew alongside their effort.

The same was true for workers with employer pensions. They showed up, did their jobs well, and committed decades to their careers. In return, the system offered predictability and dignity in retirement—not extravagance, but security.

It wasn't just discipline—it was timing.

Wages once kept pace with the cost of living. Homes cost roughly three times annual income. Pensions were common. College was affordable. It was a system that turned steady work into long-term security. That outcome is still possible today—but the climb is much steeper for younger generations.

Compare that to a millennial making $100,000 today. On the surface, it looks like success. But peel it back: They're still renting because a starter home costs $400,000. They're carrying $50,000 in student debt. Daycare is $1,500 a month. And their employer's "401(k) match" barely keeps pace with inflation.

Yes, many people in the top half worked hard and saved responsibly. But they also came of age in a system that rewarded effort with stability. Younger generations are playing a different game with different rules—and are often criticized for not winning it the same way.

WHERE WE GO FROM HERE: THE FUTURE OF INEQUALITY

Over the last forty years, Americans became more productive, more educated, and more competitive. But the gains went to the top.

Looking ahead, AI and automation will supercharge productivity even further, creating trillions in new wealth. But if history is a guide, most of it won't reach everyday workers. Without reforms in housing, healthcare, and education, we risk building an economy where wealth concentrates even more at the top while younger generations are left behind.

That's not just an economic problem—it's the unraveling of the American Dream.

The solution starts with education: teaching financial literacy and investing basics in high schools so the next generation can prioritize building assets early. It means requiring corporations to pay wages that keep pace with productivity, and even expanding stock ownership so that when companies grow, their workers grow too. Or find a way to cut federal income tax on the first $100K earned (more on that later). Because here's the hard truth: If younger generations remain locked out of homeownership and real wealth-building opportunities, retirement as we know it disappears. A "renter's economy" doesn't just mean higher monthly costs—it means millions of people reaching their later years without the safety net that home equity and savings once provided. And if that's the path we continue down, the American Dream doesn't just slip away in theory—it collapses in practice.

Chapter 9

HOW DO WE RETIRE IN A RENTER'S ECONOMY?

When I moved to Los Angeles in the summer of 2006—just three weeks after graduating high school—I did what most new actors have to do: rent. My first place was a one-bedroom apartment in Burbank that I shared with a roommate I'd met through an acting competition. To keep costs down, we split the bedroom and each paid about $500 a month.

Back then and just like today, rent in Los Angeles is higher than in most parts of the country, but it's still somewhat manageable. Over the next fifteen years, though, I bounced from apartment to apartment—seventeen different moves in total. Even when I started making good money working on *Days of Our Lives*, homeownership always felt just out of reach.

In 2013, I even tried to buy a townhouse for $419,000. That same place today is probably worth around $750,000. At the time, I couldn't qualify, and even if I could have, it would have been scary. Acting can be unpredictable, and tying myself to a mortgage never seemed safe. So I stayed a perpetual renter.

Looking back, I realize that my experience in Los Angeles was an early glimpse of what much of America would later face. Homeownership became harder to attain, while renting became the default—even for people doing well financially.

And to be fair, there are real perks to renting:

- **Flexibility.** Millennials and Gen Z value mobility—we want the freedom to explore, travel, and chase opportunities wherever they might lead. Renting lets us pick up and move without being tied down by property ownership.
- **Affordability (at first glance).** With housing prices and interest rates skyrocketing, the barrier to homeownership can feel impossible. Renting avoids massive down payments and often provides a lower monthly cost—especially early in your career.
- **Convenience.** Renters don't have to stress over repairs, maintenance, or fluctuating market values. When the dishwasher breaks, it's not your problem—it's the landlord's.

But those short-term benefits come with a long-term cost if you don't plan for retirement accordingly. Renting doesn't build equity. Paying rent for decades means you're essentially covering someone else's mortgage, not your own. And when retirement comes, renters don't have a paid-off home to fall back on.

For most Americans, their house isn't just a roof over their heads—it's their biggest financial asset. Owning a home has historically meant stability, security, and the chance to build wealth over time. You can customize it, raise a family in it, and—eventually—pass it down to your kids or grandkids. Most importantly, once the mortgage is paid off, your living expenses drop dramatically. All that's left are property taxes and insurance—a financial cushion that makes retirement far more manageable.

Without homeownership, younger generations risk losing that safety net. As we've discussed, at the time of writing this book, the combination of sky-high home prices and elevated interest rates makes ownership feel out of reach for many millennials and Gen Zers. For some, the better path right now may actually be renting—but here's the key: Renting only works long-term if you also invest. Renting without building assets could set you up for a very difficult retirement.

That's why this isn't a black-and-white conversation. There are pros and cons to both paths, and my goal is to help you see them clearly so you can make the choice that's right for you and your family.

SO SHOULD YOU RENT OR BUY A HOME?

On social media, the rent-versus-buy debate is everywhere. Some argue that renting is "throwing money away" and buying a house is the ultimate sign you've made it. One side screams, *"Stop making your landlord rich!"* and the other yells, *"Owning is a trap!"*

So what's the right move?

The answer depends on your lifestyle, financial situation, and long-term goals. Let's start with the positives of owning a home.

The first step is to shift your mindset: Don't think of a primary home as a quick investment that will make you rich. Think of it more like a *forced savings account*. Over time, a mortgage builds equity, and once it's paid off, your housing costs drop dramatically—just when you need it most, in retirement.

Consider this: A retiree in a paid-off $400,000 home might spend just $600 a month on property taxes and insurance. Meanwhile, their millennial daughter down the street could be paying $1,900 a month for a small apartment.

Now imagine if that retiree had never purchased the home. They'd also be paying $1,900 a month in rent—on a fixed income, without the cushion of equity. That's the core advantage of homeownership: stability and security.

Looking ahead, if housing and rent prices continue their historical climb, the gap could become even wider. A $400,000 home today could be worth $1 million in thirty years. The homeowner's monthly burden in retirement might be closer to $2,000 (taxes and insurance), while renters could be paying $5,000–$8,000 per month. That's a difference of $3,000–$6,000 every single month.

That's the power of homeownership. It doesn't just provide shelter—it provides stability, financial security, and an asset to pass down.

WHY YOUR PRIMARY HOME IS MORE LIKE FORCED SAVINGS THAN AN INVESTMENT

We often look back at the boomer generation and think: *Wow, they bought a house for $50,000 and now it's worth $500,000—that must have been the greatest investment ever.*

And yes, that kind of appreciation looks amazing on paper. But what we often forget is that there were decades of costs along the way. The same is true today. Historically, US home prices have grown around 4 percent a year. That means if you buy a $450,000 home today, it could be worth between $1.1 million and $1.5 million in thirty years, depending on the market. At first glance, it looks like a massive win—you "made" hundreds of thousands, maybe even close to a million dollars.

But here's the catch: Once you unpack the real costs, you'll see why I prefer to think of your primary residence less as a pure investment and more as a forced savings account.

MEET JAKE AND SOFIA

Jake and Sofia are in their early thirties. When Sofia lands a promotion, they move to a new city and spend a few weeks living out of an Airbnb. They fall in love with the job, the neighborhood, and the idea of planting roots—especially since they're planning to start a family soon.

One night over takeout and a bottle of wine, they scroll through Zillow and spot several homes in the $450,000 range. Within two weeks of touring, they find "the one." Their offer is accepted, and just like that—they're homeowners.

It's exciting, and it's a milestone. But as we'll see, owning this home is less about "striking it rich" and more about slowly, steadily building equity.

THE REAL COSTS OF JAKE AND SOFIA'S HOME

Let's look at everything Jake and Sofia can expect to pay over the thirty-year lifespan of their mortgage, including (but certainly not limited to) their original purchase and loan costs.

They put $50,000 down and borrow $400,000 at 6.5 percent. Over thirty years, they'll pay back the $400K principal plus about $500K in interest if they never refinance or make extra payments. That's **$950,000** total for just the mortgage and interest—before we add anything else.

Then, there are property taxes. At $5,000 per year, property taxes over thirty years add another **$150,000** (and realistically, that number most likely rises over time).

We can't forget insurance. At roughly $3,000 per year, that's about **$100,000** more over three decades (and realistically, that number rises over time as well).

Then there's the fact that the home must be maintained, and repairs will be needed. Experts recommend budgeting around 1 percent of the home's value per year for upkeep. Over thirty years, that's about **$200,000+**—covering things like HVAC systems, water heaters, appliances, the roof, landscaping, plumbing, and all the little fixes that come with time.

Finally, as Jake and Sofia's family grows, so do their needs and tastes. Maybe the office becomes a nursery, or they upgrade the kitchen and floors once they're further along in their careers. Over thirty years, those changes can easily total another **$200,000**.

Let's look at the big picture:

- $950,000 (mortgage + interest)
- $150,000 (taxes)
- $100,000 (insurance)
- $200,000 (maintenance and repairs)
- $200,000 (renovations and upgrades)

When you add it all up, that's **$1.6 million.**

So yes—Jake and Sofia bought a $450,000 home, and after thirty years it could be worth $1.5 million. But after all costs, they've likely spent about $1.6 million along the way.

That's why I say homeownership of your primary residence isn't the same as hitting the jackpot on an investment. It's more like a long-term savings vehicle:

- You end up with an asset worth hundreds of thousands (or millions) of dollars.
- You dramatically lower your housing costs in retirement.
- You build equity you can borrow against or pass down to your kids.

It's not "free money." But it is a disciplined, built-in way of saving—because every mortgage payment ensures that, at the end of the journey, you'll own something valuable outright.

HOW TO SAVE ON INTEREST

For Jake and Sofia, buying their $450,000 home with a $400,000 loan at 6.5 percent was a big milestone—but it doesn't mean they're stuck paying that full $500,000 in interest over the next thirty years.

Along the way, they'll have opportunities to save tens of thousands of dollars—if they play their cards right.

OPTION 1: REFINANCING IF RATES DROP

Let's say the economy shifts and mortgage rates fall to 4.5 percent. If Jake and Sofia refinanced at the right time, their monthly payment could drop significantly, and over the life of the loan they'd save a huge chunk of money in interest. Refinancing is never a one-size-fits-all solution—you'd want to carefully run the numbers with a lender—but for the right household, it can be a game changer.

OPTION 2: PAYING EXTRA TOWARD PRINCIPAL

Even if rates don't fall, Jake and Sofia can take control. By sending an extra $300 a month toward their mortgage, they'd shave off **seven years and seven months** from the life of the loan. That means being debt free almost a decade earlier—and saving nearly **$150,000** in interest. All it takes is setting up a simple automatic payment, like a subscription to their future freedom. (You can play with these numbers by going to Google and typing in "Pay off mortgage early calculator.")

OPTION 3: INVESTING INSTEAD

But here's the twist: That same $300 could take a different path. If Jake and Sofia invested $300 a month into the stock market for thirty years with an 8 percent average return (reinvesting dividends), they'd end up with roughly **$422,000**. That actually outweighs the $150,000 saved by paying off the mortgage early.

So which path is better? There's no single right answer. For some, the emotional relief of being mortgage free is priceless. For others, the math says invest the difference and let compounding work its magic. Jake and Sofia might even do a little of both: chip away at the mortgage while also building an investment portfolio.

Either way, the key is this: Small, consistent decisions—whether toward debt reduction or investing—can change the entire financial picture over the long haul.

DON'T SELL TOO EARLY

Jake and Sofia felt good about their plan—running the numbers, setting a budget, even talking about extra payments. But there's one more piece of advice I'd give them, and to anyone buying their first home: If you can, hold on to the home for at least ten to twelve years.

Why so long? Because the first decade of a mortgage is brutal. Even though Jake and Sofia's principal and interest payment is just over $2,500 a month, most of that in the early years goes straight to interest—not the principal. For example, in year one, about $2,100 of that payment is interest, while only about $400 chips away at the actual loan balance. That means their equity is growing painfully slowly.

On top of that, buying a house comes with steep up-front costs. When Jake and Sofia closed on their home, if they weren't able to get any seller concessions, they had to pay around $15,000 in fees. That's money that doesn't build equity—it's just the price of admission. And if they turned around and sold the house just three years later, they'd face another 4–6 percent in realtor commissions and closing costs on the back end. Add it all up, and even if their house appreciated a little, they might barely break even—or worse, lose money.

That's why patience is key. By holding for ten to twelve years, Jake and Sofia give themselves time to:

- Pay down a meaningful chunk of principal (so their equity grows);
- Let appreciation actually outpace those up-front and back-end costs;
- Potentially build enough equity to roll into their next home.

Of course, life happens—job changes, family needs, or emergencies can force a sale earlier. But if you can go into homeownership with the mindset of holding for at least a decade, you dramatically increase the odds of walking away with real equity in your pocket.

At the end of the day, Jake and Sofia made a smart, forward-looking decision. They bought a home that fits their long-term vision, they understand the true costs, and they've already thought about strategies to save money along the way—whether through refinancing, extra payments, or steady investing. Most importantly, they're approaching homeownership with patience, knowing that the real benefits come after a decade or more of building equity. If they stay the course, they'll not only raise their family in a home they love, but they'll also enter retirement with a powerful financial cushion.

That's the kind of outcome we want for everyone. But before you jump into strategies like extra principal payments or investing on the side, we need to take a step back and ask a more fundamental question: *Is buying a home in today's economy the right move for you?* For Jake and Sofia, the answer was yes—but the answer won't be the same for everyone. That's why I want to walk through the thought process with another couple, Tom and Lily, as they weigh the decision to buy. By going step-by-step, we'll look at the factors that can make homeownership enrich your life—rather than risk turning it into a financial trap.

HOW DO YOU KNOW IF YOU ARE READY TO BUY?

Jake and Sofia were in a position where buying made sense for them, but that won't be true for everyone. The reality is, not every purchase is going to be the right fit at the right time—and that's okay. My goal is to help you think through the decision so that, like Jake and Sofia, your home becomes a source of stability and wealth instead of stress.

To illustrate, let's meet Tom and Lily. They're excited about the idea of buying their first home, but before they make the leap, I want to walk through the questions every future homeowner should ask.

At the end of the day, two questions matter most:

1. Are you comfortable with the monthly payment?
2. Do you see yourself keeping the home for at least ten to twelve years?

If you can't confidently answer yes to both, you may want to hit pause. But even if you can, there's another key piece to consider: Can you not only *qualify* for the loan, but also *comfortably afford* the house?

THE DIFFERENCE BETWEEN QUALIFYING AND AFFORDING

When Tom and Lily sit down with their lender, the process looks straightforward. The bank checks their credit scores, verifies their employment, and runs the numbers on their debt-to-income ratio. On paper, they check all the boxes. The bank says, "Approved."

But here's the problem: Lenders don't know your lifestyle. They can't see the daycare bill you'll be paying next year, the vacations you save for every summer, or how much you love dining out on weekends. The bank doesn't know your life—it only knows your numbers. To be fair, some lenders will go beyond the formulas and talk with you about lifestyle choices, future expenses, and whether the monthly payment feels realistic. Those are the good ones—the ones looking out for your long-term financial health, not just closing the loan. But even then, remember this: Their job is to assess risk for the bank, not to be your financial planner. At the end of the day, no one knows your budget and goals better than you. That's why running your own math is non-negotiable. A home should feel like a pleasure, not a prison. If 50–60 percent of your take-home pay goes straight to housing, you're going to feel trapped. That's what people call being "house poor"—you technically qualified for the home, but after covering the mortgage and all the hidden costs, you're left with little to invest, save, or enjoy life.

LET'S ILLUSTRATE THIS

Tom and Lily together earn $100,000 a year and are considering purchasing a $415,000 home with a lower down payment of $15,000.

- **Gross income (what the lender sees):** $8,333/month
- **Mortgage + property taxes + homeowner's + private mortgage insurance:** about $3,300/month
- **Take-home pay (after taxes, health insurance, 401(k)):** $5,833/month

On paper, the bank sees the $8,333 figure and stamps the loan "Approved." But in reality, that $3,300 payment eats up nearly 57 percent of their *take-home* pay—before utilities, maintenance, or unexpected repairs. Add those in, and the burden jumps closer to 65 percent.

Can they technically qualify? Yes. But would life feel comfortable? Probably not.

WHAT WOULD MAKE IT COMFORTABLE?

For Tom and Lily, they'd need one of three things:

1. A bigger down payment to shrink the loan amount and monthly cost
2. A higher income to balance out the payment
3. A cheaper house

There are plenty of rules of thumb, but one I like is this: Aim to keep your mortgage between 25–30 percent of your take-home pay.

So in their case, with $5,833 coming in each month, a "comfortable" mortgage would be around $1,600. That's less than half of what their actual payment would be.

And here's the harsh reality: That's the conundrum millennials and Gen Z face today. In many parts of the country, you simply don't find homes in the $250,000–$300,000 range anymore. And unless you've got $100,000–$150,000 saved for a down payment on the average house, you're stuck with a loan size that pushes the monthly payment into uncomfortable territory.

And this is where the numbers really matter. A lender doesn't just look at the price tag of the house—they break everything down into monthly payments, debt ratios, and cash needed up front. Understanding how those pieces work together can mean the difference between being stretched thin—or finding a loan structure that actually supports your lifestyle. So before you start house hunting, let's walk through how lenders qualify you, why debt plays such a huge role, and what it really takes to be financially ready for a mortgage.

HOW QUALIFYING FOR A LOAN WORKS—AND WHY DEBT MATTERS

Because everyone's situation is different, it's smart to sit down with a lender months before you're ready to buy. That early meeting can uncover potential issues with cash on hand, credit score, or monthly debt payments—and give you time to fix them before you're house shopping. I saw it too often when I was an agent: A couple would be thrilled to buy, only to find out at the lender's office that they weren't financially prepared yet.

When Tom and Lily met with a lender, the first questions on the table were simple:

- What type of loan fits best for them (conventional, FHA, VA, USDA)?
- How much house could they actually afford?
- How much would they need for closing costs?

- And, most importantly, how would their monthly debt payments affect the size of the loan they could qualify for?

This last point is key. Lenders don't qualify you based on the total home price—they qualify you based on the **monthly payment**. That means property taxes, homeowner's insurance, PMI (private mortgage insurance), and HOA (homeowners' association) fees all matter as much as the sticker price on the house. For example, Tom and Lily could qualify for a $300,000 single-family home with no HOA, but not a $275,000 condo with a $700 monthly HOA fee. Same price range, totally different outcome—because the monthly numbers tell the story.

Here's a simple way to estimate where you stand: Lenders usually look at your debt-to-income ratio (DTI), which is the percentage of your gross income that goes toward debts. Depending on the loan type, that number can typically range anywhere from about 36 percent up to 50 percent. To keep things simple, let's use 40 percent as a middle ground for a rough estimate.

You take about 40 percent of your gross income and divide it by twelve. That's roughly the maximum monthly payment (including mortgage, taxes, and insurances—homeowner's and private mortgage insurance) you'll qualify for *if you have no other debt*. For example, with a $100,000 income, that works out to about $3,333 a month.

But Tom and Lily, like most people, don't live debt free. Between a $400 car payment, $300 in student loans, and $300 in credit cards, that's $1,000 a month already spoken for. So instead of qualifying for a $3,333 housing payment, their budget shrinks to around $2,333. That difference—$1,000 a month—could lower their approved loan amount by more than $100,000.

That's why sometimes paying down debt before buying can be such a game changer. Not only does it help you qualify for more, it also frees up money for the fun parts of life—travel, investing, and yes, even date nights.

And then there's the up-front cash. Even with first-time buyer programs, Tom and Lily still needed to factor in a down payment—sometimes as little as 3 percent ($12,000 on a $400,000 home)—plus closing costs, which average around 4 percent ($16,000). In some cases, sellers can agree to cover part of your closing costs, which helps ease the up-front burden. And certain loan types, like VA loans, may reduce or even eliminate some of these costs altogether. The specifics depend on your situation, which is why it's so important to review options with your lender. Add in an inspection cost, moving expenses, and a cushion for furniture or repairs, and the total easily climbs past $30,000.

On top of that, a fully funded emergency fund—three to six months of expenses—isn't mandatory, but it's just nice to have. It's the safety net that keeps a dream home from turning into a financial nightmare when life throws you a curveball.

For Tom and Lily, the takeaway was clear: The path to comfortable homeownership wasn't just about choosing the right house. It was about weighing their options, understanding the full financial picture, and making an informed decision that worked for both of them.

And here's the reality: If you're like Tom and Lily, you're not alone. Even with a strong income, many people today don't feel comfortable buying—or simply don't qualify in a way that makes sense for their budget. In that case, renting isn't a failure. Sometimes, it's the smarter move.

If you rent, you must also invest. Without the cushion of a paid-off home someday, your retirement savings become even more important. For example, if you can comfortably afford $2,200 a month for rent, consider finding a rental for $1,800 and automatically investing the extra $400 into an S&P 500 index fund. Set it up so the $400 transfers into your brokerage account the same day your rent clears. That consistency is what builds long-term wealth.

In some cases, disciplined renters can actually come out ahead of homeowners. While a homeowner might end up with a paid-off house and $2 million in retirement savings after thirty years, a renter who invests aggressively could have more. Think about it: Instead of putting $50,000–$100,000 into a down payment and closing costs, imagine that money invested in an index fund from day one. Add to that the ongoing savings from not having to cover maintenance, repairs, and remodels, plus consistent monthly contributions, and you may find your retirement account outpacing the homeowner's equity. In other words, you might not own a house, but you could own a much larger retirement portfolio—say $5 million instead of $2 million—and comfortably pay rent well into the future.

That's why, whether you buy or rent, retirement has to be at the top of your priority list. Assets are what protect you from inflation, and compound interest is what gives you freedom down the road. Which brings us to the next chapter: how to build a retirement plan that works for you.

Chapter 10

THE MILLION-DOLLAR RETIREMENT QUESTION

There's no question that retirement planning has changed dramatically.

The best way to predict the future is to look at the past. So let's take a trip back in time and meet our boomer friend, Tim.

It's 1978. Tim is twenty-four years old, working a steady job at a manufacturing company, and just bought his first home—a charming fixer-upper in a quiet cul-de-sac with sidewalks and streetlights—for $39,000. His monthly mortgage payment, taxes included, is about $250—less than 20 percent of his $1,300 monthly salary. It's manageable, leaving room in the budget for groceries, family outings, and saving. The home has a backyard, perfect for his three-year-old son and their golden retriever puppy. His wife, who is pregnant with their second child, stays home, managing the house and preparing for their growing family.

Life isn't always smooth. In his early thirties, Tim's company downsizes, and for a while he struggles to find stable work. Money gets tight. But instead of throwing in the towel, Tim makes a big decision: He goes back to college at night. Tuition is about $800 a year at the local state school—something he can cover with a side job and a few extra weekend shifts. It's grueling—working odd jobs by day, classes by evening, studying after the kids are asleep—but eventually, he earns his degree. That degree lands him a corporate job with better pay, health insurance, and something new on the horizon: retirement benefits.

One day at work, Tim hears about a brand-new program called a 401(k). Unlike many of his generation who could still rely on pensions, Tim's new company doesn't offer one. But this 401(k) idea intrigues him. That night, he rushes home, excited to tell his wife about it.

He grabs a pen, paper, and calculator and starts running the numbers.

"If I put away just $300 a month into this 401(k) for the next forty years, we could retire as millionaires!"

His wife claps her hands. The golden retriever barks, as if to celebrate with them.

So Tim makes a commitment. Even when money is tight, he contributes to his retirement account. As he climbs the corporate ladder and his pay increases, he bumps his contributions from $300 to $500 a month. By 2010, he and his wife pay off their mortgage. By 2023, Tim retires with more than $1 million tucked away in his 401(k).

And that's not all.

His once-$39,000 home is now worth a whopping $570,000. On top of that, he's receiving $2,200 a month in Social Security benefits.

At sixty-five years old, Tim is sitting on a net worth of more than $1.5 million. What started with a setback—a layoff, night school, and sacrifice—ended with a secure retirement, thanks to steady saving, homeownership, and the good fortune of living in a time when wages, housing, and education were all aligned.

THE 4 PERCENT RULE: THE GOLDEN RETIREMENT FORMULA

When Tim meets with his financial advisor, he learns about something called the **4 percent rule**—a simple strategy designed to make sure retirees don't outlive their savings.

The rule goes like this: If you withdraw only 4 percent of your retirement savings each year, your money should last at least thirty years, even with market ups and downs.

For Tim, 4 percent of his $1 million nest egg means he can safely pull out $40,000 a year—or about $3,333 a month. Add that to his $2,200 monthly Social Security check, and his retirement income is $5,533 a month.

Not bad.

Tim pulls out his notepad and calculator—just like he did forty years ago when he first ran the numbers. Housing is still his biggest expense, but with his mortgage paid off, his monthly costs (taxes, insurance) come out to about $800. Groceries, gas, and utilities total another $1,200. His Social Security check alone covers the basics. That leaves him with more than $3,000 a month for travel, hobbies, home projects, and—most importantly—spoiling the grandkids.

Tim and his wife join a pickleball league three days a week. They take trips, brunch with friends, and spend time with family. After forty-five years of work, they've arrived at the American Dream. Tim raises a glass and says, "This is what it was all about."

And he's right.

Of course, not every boomer landed where Tim did. While baby boomers collectively hold the title of the wealthiest generation in history, many don't share in that celebration. The average 401(k) balance for boomers hovers around **$250,000**—just enough to cover basic expenses if their home is paid off and they have Social Security or a pension to lean on.[65] But for those without strong pensions or extra savings, retirement often means living on a fixed Social Security check that barely covers the bills.

And in recent years, inflation, soaring housing costs, and volatile markets have eroded much of the security older Americans once counted on. Many now face the same financial pressures younger generations are feeling—just at a stage of life when stability was supposed to be the reward. That's why we're seeing more seniors take on part-time work—not for leisure, but for survival.

The truth is it wasn't always a failure of discipline. Just like today, society at large—and our government—never made financial literacy a priority. So, for many boomers, they fell into the same traps we're facing now. On top of that, the 401(k) was brand new when they were entering the workforce. Financial literacy wasn't taught in schools, employers didn't always match contributions, and plenty assumed Social Security or pensions would do the heavy lifting. And unlike us, they didn't have TikToks breaking down investing in sixty seconds, podcasts explaining financial strategies, or YouTube and ChatGPT putting knowledge in the palm of their hands. If you didn't grow up in a financially savvy household back then, you often didn't get that education at all. For some, that bet didn't pay off—and now, with less time on their side, they can't make up the gap.

This is why millennials and Gen Z need to pay close attention. Because as crushing as it feels to juggle debt, rent, and low wages right now, the one advantage we *do* have is time. If you're twenty-eight, thirty-eight, or even forty-two reading this today, you still have years ahead of you to let compounding work its magic.

But here's the bigger question: Tim's path still works—but the game board has changed. Boomers who fell short in retirement were often held back by a lack of financial education, even though wages and living costs were more in balance. Today, it's flipped: Millennials and Gen Z have more access to financial knowledge than ever, but, as we now know, wages haven't kept pace with housing, education, and everyday expenses. So what happens when Tim's grandkids try to follow the same playbook?

IF WE FOLLOWED TIM'S PATH

Meet Connor—Tim's grandson.

He's twenty-four, fresh out of college, and excited to start his career in accounting. He took the long road—six years instead of four—after switching majors, but he made it through.

The catch? He's carrying $87,000 in student loan debt.

Back at his apartment with two roommates, Connor grabs a pen, a notepad, and a calculator. "This is how Grandpa did it," he says. "If I put $300 a month into my retirement account, I'll have $1 million by the time I retire."

One roommate lights up. "Dude, you'll be a millionaire!"

Connor grins. "I'll have to drive for Uber on weekends for a while—my student loan payments are $700 a month—but once I make more, I'll bump contributions to $600. Either way, I'll be set."

But his other roommate frowns. "Wait . . . $1 million? That only gives you $40,000 a year under the 4 percent rule. That's not even enough to live on now. And in forty years?"

Connor hesitates. "Well, Social Security will help. That should rise with inflation."

"Even if it does," his roommate pushes back, "look at housing. When your grandpa was your age, his mortgage was $250. Now, the average mortgage is $3,500. Rent used to be $200; now it's $2,000 for a one-bedroom. If history repeats itself, we could be looking at $7,000 rent in forty years."

Connor opens his laptop and types into ChatGPT:

"If I want the same spending power as $1,000,000 today, how much do I need in forty years?"

The answer pops up: **$3.26 million at 3 percent annual inflation.**

Connor's eyes widen. "$3.26 million dollars?!"

His roommate leans over. "Okay, ask this—if you want $3.26 million in forty years, how much do you need to invest each month at 8 percent annual growth?"

Connor types again. The answer: **$797 a month.**

Connor slumps back in his chair. "797?! That's insane. I don't even have that after rent and student loans."

WHAT THOSE NUMBERS MEAN

Here's the reality: $1 million in forty years won't stretch the way it does today. At 3 percent inflation, prices double about every twenty-four years. (Historically, inflation has averaged closer to 3 percent a year, even though the Federal Reserve's target is 2 percent. To be cautious, we'll use 3 percent.) That means what costs you one dollar today could cost three dollars or more in forty years. So to have the *same buying power* as $1 million today, you'd need **$3.26 million in 2065.**

On the flip side, the good news is compound interest works in your favor—if you can invest consistently. At an average 8 percent annual return (which is historically what the stock market has produced over the long haul when you reinvest dividends), investing $797 a month for forty years could get you there. That's the road map Tim followed in his generation through his 401(k).

HERE'S THE HOPE

Even with all these challenges, the road map is still there. Every dollar invested in a Roth IRA, 401(k), or index fund has the power to multiply over time. Consistency matters more than perfection. For some, it may not be $797 a month at first—it might be $50, $100, or $300. But starting something, even small, is infinitely better than waiting.

Because if inflation is the enemy, compound interest is the weapon we can use to fight back. And while the old American Dream may no longer exist in the same way, a *new version* can—if we adapt, play smarter, and start stacking assets wherever we can.

And that's where we turn next: how millennials and Gen Z can actually *win* moving forward.

RETIREMENT ISN'T DEAD—BUT WE HAVE TO PLAY THE GAME DIFFERENTLY

Now, I don't want you to feel completely defeated. Yeah, the idea of needing over three million to retire sounds ridiculous—borderline cruel, even—but here's the good news: Again, we still have time. Unlike the housing crisis that's beating us down right now, retirement is still twenty, thirty, maybe even fifty years away depending on your age. That gives us room to strategize, learn, and adapt.

In the meantime, I highly recommend hopping on ChatGPT, YouTube, or Google to explore how to start investing—even if it's just $100 a month. Once you've done your research, verify your approach with a trusted financial professional. It's not about getting rich overnight; it's about getting momentum on your side. I'll break down a bunch of practical options in the final chapter, but I wanted to leave you with some hope here—because the last thing I want is for you to throw your hands up, order a large stuffed-crust pizza, and eat it over the kitchen sink in defeat. (Though, to be fair, that does sound kind of amazing right now.)

But here's the brutal difference between Tim's generation and ours: Their work structure made retirement easier. Boomers often spent decades at the same company, slowly moving up the ranks, collecting steady pay raises, health benefits, and eventually retiring with either a pension or a fat 401(k) match. Stability was baked into the system.

Us? We're job-hopping every few years just to get a cost-of-living raise. We're freelancing, side hustling, and navigating the gig economy because companies no longer invest in their employees the way they once did. That means many of us don't get 401(k) matches, stable health insurance, or any kind of long-term financial security. And while "working for yourself" sounds glamorous, the reality is that it makes retirement even harder—you are responsible for 100 percent of your future. No pension. No company match. No safety net unless you build it.

And let's be honest—when you're already saddled with student loans, high rent, and a car payment, putting thousands away for the distant future feels almost impossible. That's why so many people today can't even imagine retirement. The "retirement age" used to be sixty-five. Now? For many, even seventy is starting to look optimistic.

But here's the good news: If you're in your thirties or forties and still wrestling with debt, it's not too late. Your path just looks different. I know this because my wife and I were in the same boat. For years, we carried a heavy load of debt that made investing feel out of reach. But we attacked it, one bill at a time. When we finally paid off the credit cards, we freed up nearly $1,000 a month. Suddenly, the money that used to vanish into debt payments could stay in our pockets. That makes the 401(k) contributions much more doable now.

That's the key shift. Debt repayment isn't just about relief—it's about opportunity. Every time you eliminate a monthly payment, you create future wealth. That $500 car payment? Redirected into a Roth IRA, it could grow into hundreds of thousands over twenty-five years. That $300 student loan? That's a future index fund investment compounding on your behalf. Progress compounds, and once you clear the debt hurdle, the same forces that worked for Tim can finally start working for you.

But here's where the shift in mindset comes in. Retirement isn't impossible—it just means we have to play a different game than previous generations did. For us, it's about:

- **Investing earlier,** even if it's just small amounts in index funds.
- **Building multiple income streams**—side hustles, businesses, freelancing—that can grow alongside your career.
- **Avoiding lifestyle inflation** and keeping expenses in check.

- **Leveraging real estate (if possible)** to create stability later in life.

The rules of the game have changed, but that doesn't mean the game is unwinnable. No one is coming to save us, but if we think differently, adapt, and start building momentum now, we can still create a future where work is a choice, not a necessity.

Because at the end of the day, retirement isn't about "quitting." It's about freedom. Freedom to work because you want to, not because you have to. Freedom to travel, spend time with family, or even play pickleball three times a week like Tim.

And maybe—just maybe—we won't be delivering DoorDash orders at seventy-five just to pay rent.

Chapter 11

WORK-LIFE BALANCE

How is it possible that the nine-to-five corporate job still exists in 2025? Back in the day, it made sense. We didn't have today's tech innovations to make work faster and more productive. People could live ten minutes from their office instead of being pushed forty-five minutes out of the city just to find an affordable place to live. The "nine-to-five" was never really nine to five anyway—it was (and still is) closer to eight to six once you add commuting, getting ready, dropping off kids, and the rest of life's logistics. Factor in a lunch break and you're really talking closer to sixty hours a week tied to your job.

And that's if you're lucky enough to only need *one* job. For a lot of millennials and Gen Z, the "traditional" workweek doesn't even account for the serving shifts, freelance gigs, or side hustles we pick up just to keep pace with rent and bills. The nine-to-five isn't just outdated—it's unsustainable.

Let's meet Natalie.

Natalie was making six figures at a corporate job, but her day-to-day reality looked nothing like the picture of "success." Every morning she woke up at six to iron her clothes, put on makeup, get dressed, and crawl through an hour of traffic to get to the office. By the time she sat down at her desk, she was already exhausted—and her inbox was overflowing with "urgent" emails. At five, she'd repeat the process in reverse, crawling home through bumper-to-bumper traffic, pulling into her driveway closer to 7 PM. If she could afford to live closer to work, she would have—but housing in the city was astronomical.

When the pandemic hit and she started working from home, Natalie suddenly gained back three hours a day. That's fifteen hours a week or seven hundred and fifty hours a year just from cutting out the grind of commuting and office prep. At her $100,000 salary, those "unpaid" hours were worth nearly $40,000 a year. Instead of sitting in traffic, she could spend her evenings with family, exercise, and invest her extra energy into a side hustle that brought in a few hundred extra dollars a month.

And she wasn't just saving time—she was saving money. No more gas, tolls, expensive work clothes, or twelve-dollar lunches. That money went toward home repairs, paying down debt, and actually building stability.

Natalie was happier. Healthier. Less stressed. For the first time, she felt like she was *living* instead of just grinding.

So when her company eventually told her that returning to the office was the only way to "get ahead," Natalie didn't even blink. Why would she trade thirty full days of her life each year for a 3 percent raise and free Chick-fil-A Fridays? The math didn't add up. If they forced her back, she was ready to quit.

Loyalty works both ways. Companies love to talk about "commitment" and "team culture," but they rarely acknowledge the time and money workers spend just to show up. If employers want loyalty, they need to respect their employees' lives—by offering fair pay, flexibility, and benefits that actually offset the hidden costs of working.

And Natalie was lucky. Her job *could* be done remotely. Millions of workers don't have that option. Mechanics, nurses, retail employees, restaurant workers—they can't log in from home. But that doesn't mean they should be chained to outdated schedules that eat their lives alive.

Because the point isn't that everyone should work from home. The point is that all of us—remote or not—deserve a system that respects our time. Technology has made us more productive than ever, but instead of benefiting from that progress and higher wages, we're still stuck grinding through five (or six) days a week just to survive.

That's why the four-day workweek matters. Not just for people like Natalie, but for everyone. It's not about slacking off—it's about finally rebalancing the equation so life isn't squeezed into the margins of work.

THE FOUR-DAY WORKWEEK SHOULD HAVE EXISTED YEARS AGO

We've been so gaslit as a society that we're literally fighting for the "privilege" of working only forty hours a week and surviving on one job per person. That's the goal right now—not having to grind sixty-plus hours just to scrape by.

But here's the bigger question: Why aren't we all working four-day weeks already?

Let's zoom out. Our grandparents' generation often thrived in single-income households. One parent—usually the dad—worked forty or fifty hours a week, bought a home on that salary, and supported a spouse who stayed home to raise three kids. That meant the total working hours per household could sit around fifty a week.

Now fast-forward to today. Despite massive leaps in technology, automation, and efficiency tools, the average household now needs *two full-time jobs* just to cover the basics.

That's a combined 100 to 120 hours of labor per week—and still, many families can't afford a home, childcare drains another $1,200–$2,000 a month, and vacations feel like luxuries reserved for the wealthy.

So how did we go from fifty hours of household labor to one hundred and twenty hours—while ending up worse off?

BURNOUT ISN'T LAZINESS—IT'S ECONOMIC EXHAUSTION

Here's the narrative we've been fed by some folks in our society: Millennials and Gen Z are lazy. We don't want to work. We're entitled.

But let's be honest: If laziness were the issue, we wouldn't have millions of people juggling two jobs, gig work, freelancing, and side hustles just to make ends meet. Laziness doesn't drive an Uber until midnight. Laziness doesn't run an Etsy shop on weekends or deliver DoorDash after working all day.

We're not lazy. We're burned out.

Picture this: You work fifty hours a week for five years. That's roughly 12,500 hours of labor. At the end of those five years, you've earned maybe $300,000–$400,000 total. On paper, that sounds like a lot. But after taxes, rent, student loans, groceries, car payments, insurance, and rising costs of literally everything, you're not sitting on a pile of wealth. You're staring at a bank account with little to no savings—and in many cases, you're still in debt.

That's not laziness. That's economic exhaustion.

And it's not just about money. It's about what the lack of money does to your life. It delays families. It defers dreams. It puts relationships under constant strain. How do you start thinking about kids when daycare costs as much as rent? How do you build wealth when buying a home requires a down payment bigger than your entire savings account?

I used to live in an apartment complex where kids didn't play in yards—they played in the hallways, on cold concrete floors. Not because their parents didn't work hard, but because homeownership was simply out of reach. That's what burnout looks like. Not an unwillingness to work, but the crushing weight of a system that demands more and gives less.

A FOUR-DAY WORKWEEK IS MORE THAN POSSIBLE—IT'S INEVITABLE

The solution isn't complicated. We don't need to reinvent the wheel. We just need to evolve the workweek to match the world we actually live in.

A shorter workweek isn't a fantasy. It's already been tested—and it works.

- In the **UK's largest four-day workweek trial** in 2022, companies reported a 35 percent boost in productivity. Employees weren't just maintaining output—they were exceeding it. Meanwhile, stress levels dropped, burnout eased, and workers reported feeling healthier and happier.[66]
- In **Iceland**, large-scale trials of a four-day workweek were so successful that nearly 90 percent of the workforce now has access to reduced or more flexible working hours. Productivity held steady or improved, while workers reported better health, lower stress, and a stronger work-life balance.[67]
- Even corporate giants have tested this. **Microsoft Japan** ran a four-day week and saw productivity spike 40 percent. Employees used less electricity, made fewer copies (fewer meetings + less busy work = less paper use), and got more done in less time. The company spent less, workers lived more.[68]

Notice the pattern? Every time the four-day week is tried, it works—for workers *and* for companies.

WHY HASN'T THIS HAPPENED YET?

If the evidence is so overwhelming, why are we still grinding away five days a week?

The truth is productivity has exploded—but wages haven't.

Back in the 1950s, the average American worker was far less productive. Offices ran on typewriters, factories depended on slow manual labor, and sending a memo meant physically walking it across the building.

Today? A Tesla rolls off the assembly line every forty-five seconds. An accountant can balance ledgers in minutes with QuickBooks. A retail system tracks every single sale in real time. Automation, software, and now AI have completely transformed the workplace. We are producing more, faster, and with fewer people.

Since 1978, worker productivity has risen roughly 60–70 percent. Over that same period, CEO pay exploded by more than 1,000 percent, while typical workers saw only about 26 percent growth.[69] The wealth created by our labor didn't vanish—it was captured at the top.

If companies had shared those gains, we wouldn't be debating a four-day workweek in 2025. It would already be the norm. Every new leap in efficiency should have meant fewer hours for workers at the same pay, freeing us to spend more time with families, to live healthier, fuller lives. Instead, corporations pocketed the difference and told us to be grateful for pizza parties and 3 percent raises.

The result is a system where we're exponentially more productive than our grandparents—but still shackled to a 1920s work schedule.

Nearly a century ago, economist John Maynard Keynes predicted that technological progress would allow people in advanced economies to work as little as **fifteen hours a week** by now.[70] Most of us would happily settle for thirty-two.

Instead, two-income households became mandatory. Wages stagnated. Housing and healthcare costs exploded. Rather than scaling down hours as productivity soared, workers were pushed to hustle harder. Instead of sharing prosperity, companies preached "loyalty" while laying people off at the first dip in quarterly profits.

This is the crossroads we're approaching again. As artificial intelligence accelerates productivity even further, the question isn't whether we *can* work less—it's whether the gains will finally be shared, or once again concentrated at the top.

We were sold the myth that struggle is character building, that working yourself into the ground is honorable. But here's the reality: Burnout isn't a badge of honor—it's a symptom of a broken system.

We're facing a new reality. And in this reality, clinging to a five-day workweek is holding us back. The data is clear: Shorter weeks mean better productivity, lower costs, healthier workers, and stronger families.

The question is, why are we still waiting for the four-day workweek? We should be living it.

Most of us are caught in a strange in-between. Do we chase the dream of "making it big"—or do we unplug, buy a tiny cabin by a lake, grow a garden, and raise chickens? Too many of us are stuck in the middle, grinding away, and that middle is where the frustration lives.

We should give ourselves credit. A forty-year narrative collapsed in front of us, and we're still standing. The internet opened our eyes, connected us, and gave us permission to rethink everything—what success means, what happiness is, what kind of life we want to build.

Because what do we really want? To actually *live*. To spend more time with people we love. To grow intellectually and spiritually. To work, yes—but as something we *do*, not as the center of our existence.

Right now, it feels like we live to work, and if we're lucky, we get scraps of life on the side. It's no wonder so many of us feel numb. We grew up believing consumerism was happiness—bigger houses, newer cars, shinier toys. And for some, that dream still matters, and that's great. But now that the price tag requires our entire lives, more and more of us are realizing it just isn't worth it.

What's worth it is progress. Freedom. Connection. Joy. That's what the next era of work should give us. Not another decade of burnout.

And maybe, just maybe, this isn't the collapse of the American Dream. Maybe it's the rebirth of a new one.

Chapter 12

HOW BILLIONAIRES AND CORPORATIONS OPERATE IN A BROKEN SYSTEM

We often hear the chant "Tax the Rich" bouncing around the internet, at protests, or even stitched in bold red letters on representative Alexandria Ocasio-Cortez's famous Met Gala dress in 2021. The sentiment is clear: People are frustrated.

And how could they not be? The distribution of wealth in America today is absurd. The top 1 percent—about 3.5 million people—hold roughly $50 trillion in wealth.[71] Meanwhile, the bottom 50 percent—about 175 million people—are left to split just $4.2 trillion.[72] That gap isn't just a statistic; it's the reason why buying a home feels impossible, why retirement savings are scarce, and why "tax the rich" has become more than a slogan—it's a cry for fairness.

Some lawmakers today champion the idea of raising the top federal income tax rate, pointing to history as their case study. And it's true—there was a time when America's richest paid far more. In the mid-twentieth century, the top marginal tax rate peaked at over 90 percent—but only on income above what would be about $2 million per year in today's dollars. The ultrarich were still rich, but the system ensured they gave back a much larger share than they do now.

So, would raising today's top tax rate make a difference? Some—but not a ton. For example, in 2024, presidential candidate Kamala Harris proposed restoring the top marginal income tax rate from 37 percent to 39.6 percent for incomes above $400,000, a change that the Tax Policy Center estimates would raise about $170.5 billion over the next decade.[73] That would generate revenue, yes—but nowhere near enough to close America's multitrillion-dollar fiscal gaps. And just as important, it would raise that money from the wrong group.

The people most exposed to higher income taxes aren't billionaires with complex asset structures; they're high-earning professionals—doctors, lawyers, small-business owners, engineers. People whose wealth shows up on W-2s and K-1s, not balance sheets. The ultrawealthy, by contrast, tend to take relatively little income at all. Their money lives in assets, not paychecks (more on this shortly), which means modest changes to income tax rates barely register for them.

In theory, higher rates mean more tax revenue. In practice, it's not transformative.

Especially when you stack it against these numbers.

In 2022 alone, S&P 500 companies spent roughly $922 billion buying back their own stock—nearly a trillion dollars redirected to shareholders in a single year.[74] At the same time, the federal government is now spending around $1 trillion every year just to service the interest on its existing debt, before a single dollar goes toward roads, schools, healthcare, or tax relief. And hovering over all of it is a $37 trillion national debt that continues to grow, quietly compounding the problem.

That's why the debate has shifted toward other solutions: taxing stock buybacks, closing the step-up in basis loophole, or even introducing a minimum tax on unrealized gains. Because if you only raise income taxes, you end up taxing the wrong people—while the real centers of wealth remain largely untouched.

But back then, the whole system was different since most wealthy people *still relied on salaries or dividends* as their main income, because the modern scale of billionaire-level stock-based wealth just wasn't as developed yet. Over the decades, policies and loopholes have been engineered so that the ultrawealthy often pay far less than the official rates suggest. They don't take home salaries like you and I do—they live off stocks, assets, and financial maneuvers that sidestep traditional income taxes.

And on one hand, you can't fault them for using the rules available to them. None of us like to see our paycheck shrink after taxes. But here's the difference: When a family earning $60,000 gets taxed, that money could have made the difference that allowed them to afford childcare, save for retirement, or finally breathe easier at the grocery store. When someone earning $5 million loses $2 million to higher taxes, their life doesn't change. They're still flying privately, sending their kids to elite schools, investing in businesses, and living in sprawling mansions.

They don't feel it.

That's why this debate matters. Not because people hate success, but because the rules of the game no longer apply equally—and the middle class is paying the price.

If the cost of living hadn't skyrocketed over the past two decades, most of us probably wouldn't care as much. If a typical forty-hour-a-week job paying $50–$60K still covered a modest home, a reliable car, childcare that didn't bankrupt you, basic healthcare, and a $500 drip into retirement, we'd have kept our heads down and called it fair.

But that deal collapsed. Costs exploded. Wages stagnated. And while the middle got squeezed, the escalators kept moving up—for the very top.

And here's the truth: Billionaires, a thriving middle class, and the elimination of poverty could absolutely coexist. America is the richest country in the world. The resources are there. We as a country could all be thriving and cheering billionaires on for driving progress, innovation, and making all our lives better. But instead, too many corporations prioritize profits over people, and that's the most frustrating part. Why with all this power and money can't you just pay people more? And it's not like we don't have companies that do it right and show us it's possible.

Take Publix, for example. Publix (privately owned) is the largest employee-owned company in America. Full- and part-time employees are eligible to receive company stock through an employee stock ownership plan (ESOP), which means the longer you work there, the more of the company you literally own. Over time, some Publix associates retire as millionaires—not because they won the lottery, but because the company shared its growth with its people.[75]

Or look at Costco (publicly owned). The average hourly wage for a Costco worker is around $30 an hour (well above the US retail average), and the company provides healthcare benefits to both full- and part-time employees. Costco's turnover rate is famously low because they treat workers as assets rather than costs. Even Wall Street analysts have acknowledged that Costco's model proves you can pay workers well, keep prices low, and still turn a profit.[76]

So if companies like Publix and Costco can do it—and still stay profitable—why can't all big corporations follow suit? The only conclusion is that they *choose* not to. They want more for themselves and less for us.

That's the heart of it. Billionaires aren't cheating the system; most are playing by the rules. But the rules themselves are designed in their favor. They don't just allow billionaires to win—they allow them to consolidate power. Power over politics. Power over media. Power over the jobs we work.

So how do billionaires and corporations keep such a tight grip on wealth while the average worker struggles to pay rent?

It comes down to a handful of strategies:

1. Borrowing against their assets (the closest thing to a personal money-printing machine);

2. Political influence (Super PACs and dark money);
3. Lobbying (to get the rules rewritten in their favor);
4. Duty to shareholders (a Supreme Court ruling that shifted power away from workers);
5. Stock buybacks (a legalized wealth transfer to the rich);
6. Tax avoidance (through shell companies and offshore loopholes).

Let's walk through these moves one by one—and see how billionaires operate on a completely different playing field than the rest of us.

BORROWING AGAINST THEIR ASSETS: THEY DON'T GET PAID LIKE US

Most ultrawealthy people don't take big paychecks at all. They hold wealth as assets—stocks, companies, real estate. That's why the proposition of raising income taxes on the rich barely grazes them.

In recent years, some of the wealthiest corporate executives in America have taken little to no traditional salary, even as their personal wealth exploded on paper. Their compensation didn't come through paychecks; it came through stock and stock options that soared in value as their companies grew. No sale, no "income." No income, no income tax.

This isn't unusual, and it isn't accidental. It's a well-established playbook. Many founders and top executives structure their compensation to minimize taxable income while allowing wealth to compound through assets. And to be clear, they aren't breaking the law. They're using the system exactly as it's written.

That's the point. When wealth is built and held primarily through assets rather than wages, the traditional income tax system barely touches it. Which is why focusing solely on income taxes misses the real engine of modern wealth—and why any serious conversation about fairness has to look beyond the tax code we already have and toward reforms that reflect how wealth is actually created today.

So how do you fund mansions, jets, investments, and political donations if you aren't "earning"?

You have two options. You can sell shares, trigger capital gains taxes, and give up future upside. Or you can borrow against those shares—pay relatively low interest, keep the stock, and owe no income tax at all.

Guess which one wins.

That borrow-against-assets strategy is the backbone of the ultrawealthy wealth machine. It even has a nickname: "buy, borrow, die." Buy appreciating assets. Borrow against them for cash instead of selling. And when you die, your heirs receive a tax reset, known as the *step-up in basis*—that can wipe out capital gains taxes entirely. It's legal. It's elegant. And it keeps compounding.

BRADLEY VERSUS MELISSA: TWO DIFFERENT GAMES

Bradley is a billionaire. He holds $500 million in stock. He wants $100 million in cash. Easy. He pledges a slice of his stock as collateral and borrows at, say, 2 percent. No sale, no capital gains, no income tax. Meanwhile, if his $500 million stockpile rises just 10 percent, his net worth grows by $50 million in a single year.

He pays the bank only $2 million in interest, keeps all his shares, and can borrow again tomorrow. That $2 million doesn't go back into schools or infrastructure—it goes straight into the bank's profits. So the banks make money, Bradley gets his cash tax free, and nothing flows into the system the rest of us depend on.

Now, Bradley and many other ultrarich will use this method to fund their lifestyle—buy a mansion, a yacht, or private jets—or buy businesses. Yes, they are avoiding taxes, but that wouldn't directly touch the rest of us as much. But he often uses that liquidity to scoop up scarce assets like housing.

Here's where it hurts. With billions in untaxed cash, a wealthy individual like Bradley and private equity firms often use this method to invest in a REIT (real estate investment trust) that buys homes as "investments." When they do this, it contributes to the climb of housing prices. The same house that went for $350,000 sells for $450,000 a few years later.

For Melissa, a physical therapy assistant, who grew up in this town, that's devastating. She finally reaches the point where she can afford a home near her parents. But instead of $350,000, that house now costs $450,000. The monthly mortgage jumps from around $2,600 to $3,300. That extra $700 a month isn't just rent—it's lost opportunity. Money that could've gone to retirement savings or her kids' college fund is now funneled upward to banks and investors.

Now imagine this: If Melissa's payment was $2,600, she could take the other $700 and invest it in the stock market. In thirty years, (with an 8 percent annual return and reinvesting her dividends) that could grow *more than a million dollars in retirement savings, and her house would be paid off*. That's the American Dream as it should be. But instead, the math now requires Melissa to come up with $4,000 a month to chase the same outcome.

And it doesn't stop with housing. The interest on bigger mortgages flows upward to lenders and investors—just like student loans at 8 percent, car loans at 9 percent, and credit cards at 20 percent. We are debt financing everyday life, while those at the top collect interest like rent on time itself.

This isn't happening in some smoky back room. It's written right into the tax code—and bragged about in quarterly earnings calls.

But the "buy, borrow, die" playbook isn't reserved for billionaires. In theory, regular folks can tap into it too—by borrowing against home equity or even taking a loan against a stock portfolio. The difference is that when we do it, the stakes are smaller, the interest rates are higher, and the risks can wipe us out if something goes wrong. For the ultrawealthy, it's nearly risk free, with cheap loans backed by assets that only seem to grow in value.

So how do we make the system more fair without taking tools away from ordinary families? One option would be to tax borrowing against assets once it passes a certain threshold—say millions, not thousands—so a family using a $50,000 home equity line to pay for college isn't punished, but a billionaire pulling out $100 million to dodge income tax is finally on the hook. Another solution is closing the "step-up in basis," which allows heirs to inherit assets like stock or real estate without paying taxes on decades of gains. Instead of wealth disappearing from the tax system forever, those gains could finally contribute to the common good. And some experts suggest implementing a minimum tax on wealth or unrealized gains, ensuring that the ultrarich can't live tax free year after year just because their income doesn't look like ours.

The point isn't to end borrowing against assets—it's to design rules that let everyone use the system fairly. Families should still be able to tap their home equity to get ahead, but billionaires shouldn't be able to live, invest, and pass on fortunes without contributing back. Fix those loopholes, and suddenly "buy, borrow, die" stops being a cheat code for the 1 percent—and becomes a system where everyone plays by the same rules.

And keep in mind that tax avoidance doesn't just happen on paper. It buys influence. Once billionaires have preserved their fortunes tax free, the next move is making sure the political system never threatens that setup. Enter Super PACs.

SUPER PACS AND DARK MONEY: HOW BILLIONAIRES BUY THE GOVERNMENT

I've made it this far without bringing politics into it, but on the issue of Super PACs, we've got to face the truth: Billionaires and corporations having unlimited money to spend on elections is a massive abuse of power. In many ways, it undermines our democracy itself.

Politics matter because they set the rules of the game. If we want economic policies that work for everyone—not just corporations—we need leaders who are accountable to the people, not to billionaires cutting checks in the shadows.

American politics has always been messy—but in 2010, one Supreme Court case supercharged the corruption: *Citizens United v. FEC*. With a single decision, the court didn't just open the door to big money in politics. They blew the hinges clean off.

Before *Citizens United*, there were limits on how much corporations and billionaires could spend on elections. After? No limits. Suddenly, politics became an all-you-can-buy buffet for the ultrawealthy.

Here's how it works. Imagine a billionaire—let's call him Mr. Monopoly. He wants lower corporate taxes. Instead of slipping a briefcase of cash to a senator (illegal), he funnels $50 million into a Super PAC. That Super PAC then blankets the airwaves with attack ads against any politician who threatens higher corporate taxes.

The ads scream: "*Candidate X wants to destroy small businesses!*" They flood the airwaves during election season, trying to scare and persuade voters. Next time an election rolls around, pay close attention. If a commercial is actually funded by the candidate, you'll hear the familiar line: "*I'm [Name], and I approve this message.*" But the darker, fear-mongering ads—the ones warning that some candidate will ruin your life—end differently. Listen closely and you'll catch it: "*This message was paid for by Americans for Prosperity and Freedom PAC.*" Sounds patriotic, right? But behind that shiny name is usually a handful of billionaires pulling the strings.

And it gets sketchier.

Enter *dark money*. Thanks to loopholes, billionaires and corporations don't even have to put their names on the checks. They funnel money through nonprofit "social welfare" groups—501(c)(4)s—or business leagues: 501(c)(6)s. These nonprofits aren't required to disclose their donors. From there, the money flows into Super PACs—which spend it on campaigns.

The result? We don't know who's bankrolling which politicians. It's a shadowy web of cash with zero accountability.

And since *Citizens United*, the floodgates have stayed wide open. In the 2023–2024 election cycle alone, Super PACs raised billions from donors—ranging from corporations and unions to "dark money" nonprofits. Of that, about $2.7 billion has already been spent by Super PACs in the form of independent expenditures. That's the technical term for money spent to influence an election without officially coordinating with a candidate's campaign. In practice, it allows wealthy donors to bankroll TV ads, mailers, digital campaigns, and even large-scale events that explicitly support or oppose candidates—while remaining legally separate from the campaigns themselves.[77]

And most of that billionaire money? It isn't spent building up candidates. It's spent tearing others down. Super PACs thrive on negativity. A big chunk of their money is used to flood TV, radio, and social media with attack ads designed to divide, scare, and polarize. Our political system becomes a nonstop mud-wrestling match—while the real winners are the billionaires pulling the strings.

This isn't just corruption. It's exclusion. Ordinary people are being priced out of democracy itself.

Because in a system where billionaires can spend unlimited money in secret, the rest of us don't get a voice. We just get the bill.

If we want real economic change, we have to tackle the political machinery that enables corruption—and that means banning Super PACs. A healthy democracy depends on citizens having an equal voice, no matter their bank account. But right now, billionaires can shout through megaphones while ordinary Americans are barely heard.

It doesn't have to be this way. We can push for reforms that overturn *Citizens United,* demand transparency for every political dollar spent, and set strict limits on outside campaign funding. Imagine an election where candidates compete on ideas, not who has the richest billionaire backer. Where every voter—teacher, truck driver, nurse, small-business owner—has the same voice at the ballot box.

That's the promise of democracy. And until we stop letting Super PACs and dark money buy our elections, that promise will stay broken.

If Super PACs decide who gets into office, lobbying decides what those officials do once they're there. And the money trail is even bigger.

LOBBYING: LEGALIZED INFLUENCE FOR SALE

Now that we've seen the power of Super PACs, let's talk about another tool corporations and billionaires use to bend the system in their favor: lobbying. If Super PACs buy elections, lobbying buys the laws that follow.

Lobbying has been part of American politics since the very beginning. The term itself comes from the nineteenth century, when lobbyists would literally wait in the lobbies of hotels and the US Capitol to corner politicians and pitch their interests. Back then, it was mostly railroad tycoons, bankers, and oil barons fighting to protect their monopolies. Today, the setting is sleeker—K Street in Washington, DC—but the game hasn't changed. It's still about who has the money to get a politician's ear.

Here's how it works. Let's say Big Pharma wants to stop a bill that would allow Medicare to negotiate lower drug prices. Instead of hoping for the best, they hire an army of lobbyists—former members of Congress, lawyers, PR experts—to wine and dine lawmakers, draft "model" legislation, and push talking points straight into political speeches. Sometimes, lobbyists even *write the bills themselves*—and the politicians just rubber-stamp them.

Imagine you're a newly elected member of Congress. You've just arrived in Washington, full of energy and ideas about serving the people back home. But within weeks, reality hits. You're told you'll need to raise tens of thousands of dollars every single week just to stay competitive for reelection.

Enter the lobbyists. They don't slide envelopes of cash across the table—that would be illegal. Instead, they offer something more valuable: access to an entire network of donors, industry groups, and PACs ready to fund your next campaign. A friendly lobbyist leans in and says: *"Support this bill, and I'll make sure the right people have your back."* Suddenly, raising campaign cash doesn't feel so impossible anymore.

But the money is just the start. Congress churns through thousands of pages of legislation every year. You and your small staff can't possibly read, let alone write, all of it. Lobbyists step in with "helpful" talking points, pre-drafted amendments, even entire bills—polished and ready to go. All you have to do is put your name on it. It saves time, but it also means the very industries you're supposed to regulate are the ones writing the rules.

And then there's the future to think about. Political careers don't last forever, and everyone in Washington knows it. Lobbyists whisper promises of cushy jobs once you leave office—consulting gigs, board seats, or a million-dollar salary lobbying your old colleagues. Play ball with Big Pharma today, and tomorrow you could be on their payroll.

Of course, there are perks in the moment too. Lobbyists represent powerful industries—oil, defense, tech, banking. Align with them, and you gain access to elite dinners, insider briefings, and political allies who make you look like a heavyweight player in DC. Refuse them, and you risk being outspent, attacked in ads, or shut out of critical networks.

So here's the blunt truth:

- Super PACs buy who gets into office.
- Lobbying buys what they do once they're there.

That's why corporations and interest groups pour more than *$4 billion a year* into lobbying.[78] Not to run campaign ads—that's what Super PACs are for—but to shape the day-to-day governing: writing the bills, influencing the regulations, funding the "research," and even creating fake grassroots movements to sway public opinion.

The result? A system where lawmakers are less accountable to voters back home and more accountable to the lobbyists who hold the keys to their money, their legislation, and even their future careers.

That's the power of lobbying. It's not a shadowy backroom deal in some movie. It's right out in the open, perfectly legal, and deeply woven into how our government works. Billionaires and corporations don't need to bribe politicians with envelopes of cash when they can hire polished lobbyists to hand deliver their policies, already gift wrapped, to Congress.

SO HOW DO WE FIX THIS?

We don't have to accept lobbying as the cost of doing business in Washington. Other democracies limit or outright ban corporate lobbying, and we could too.

First, we could close the revolving door—no more members of Congress leaving office on Friday and showing up Monday morning as a million-dollar lobbyist. A mandatory cooling-off period of five to ten years would cut off that pipeline of favors.

Second, we could require total transparency. Every meeting with a lobbyist, every draft bill they provide, every dollar spent on influence should be logged and made public. If lobbyists are shaping our laws, the public deserves to see it.

Third, we could limit corporate lobbying spending—cap what industries can spend each year or ban certain practices like lobbyists writing legislation.

And most importantly, we need public financing of elections. If candidates can run competitive campaigns with money from the people, not corporate donors, they'll be far less dependent on the lobbyists waiting in the wings.

Instead of candidates depending on massive donations from corporations, billionaires, or Super PACs, the government provides funding for political campaigns—using taxpayer dollars—so candidates can run competitive races without selling themselves to the highest bidder.

HOW IT WORKS IN PRACTICE

There are a few different models of how this could work in the real world.

- **Matching funds:** Small-dollar donations from regular citizens (say $20) get matched by the government at a multiple (like six to one). So your $20 becomes $140 for the candidate. This encourages politicians to seek support from ordinary people instead of big donors.
  Example: New York City has a program like this for local elections.[79]
- **Vouchers or "democracy dollars":** Every citizen gets a set amount (like $50 or $100 in vouchers) to donate to candidates of their choice. That way, everyone has a voice in campaign funding, not just the wealthy.
  Example: Seattle has a "Democracy Voucher" program that does exactly this.[80]
- **Full public grants:** Candidates who qualify (by gathering a certain number of small donations to show support) receive a flat grant from the government to run their campaign. In exchange, they agree not to raise big private donations.
  Example: Maine and Arizona have experimented with this model.[81]

WHY IT MATTERS

Right now, candidates spend huge chunks of their time fundraising from wealthy donors and corporations—which inevitably shapes their priorities. With public financing:

- Candidates could spend more time listening to voters, not lobbyists;
- Regular people's small donations would carry real weight;
- Corporate lobbyists would lose their grip on the system, because politicians wouldn't *need* their money to survive politically.

In short: Public financing levels the playing field. It shifts elections from "who has the richest friends" to "who has the broadest support from the people."

Because at the end of the day, democracy is supposed to mean one person, one vote—not one lobbyist, one law. Until we curb the power of lobbying, policies will continue to tilt toward corporations and billionaires, leaving ordinary Americans on the sidelines.

And why does this lobbying work so well? Because the legal foundation already tilts the playing field. A hundred-year-old court case, *Dodge v. Ford*, hardwired into corporate America that shareholder profits matter above all else.

DUTY TO SHAREHOLDERS: THE SUPREME COURT CASE THAT MADE CORPORATIONS HEARTLESS

I first heard about this case from my friend Zachary Foust, when he made a social media post about this. It opened my eyes to why corporations prioritize profits over people. It's literally baked into the law and taught in business school.

Picture this: It's the early 1900s. The Ford Motor Company is on fire—cars rolling off assembly lines, profits pouring in, and Henry Ford himself is one of the richest men in America. But Ford had a radical idea, one that could've reshaped capitalism in this country forever.

He looked at the empire he'd built and thought: *What good is all this money if the people who make it possible—the workers—can't share in the success?*

So Ford laid out a plan:

- **Cut car prices** so more Americans could afford them;
- **Raise worker wages** so his employees could live with dignity and, yes, even buy the very cars they were building.

Sounds visionary, right? A win-win for workers and customers alike.

But not everyone saw it that way. Among Ford's shareholders were the Dodge brothers (yes, those Dodge brothers, who would go on to start their own car company). They weren't interested in Ford's dream of building a stronger middle class. They wanted one thing: bigger profits in their pockets.

So they sued him.

And in 1919, in *Dodge v. Ford Motor Co.*, the court sided with the Dodges. The ruling was clear and cold: A corporation's primary duty is to its shareholders—not its workers, not its customers, not society. Just the investors.

That single decision didn't just change Ford Motor Company. It set the tone for every major corporation that followed. It locked in a legal precedent that said maximizing stock price is the only game that matters.

Want to know why companies slash jobs during record profits? Why wages flatline while CEO pay explodes? Why employees get crumbs while Wall Street gets a feast?

It all goes back to that moment—a hundred years ago—when the courts decided corporations didn't have a heart.

After the court sided with the Dodge brothers, American capitalism took a permanent turn toward *profits first, people second.* And yes, this case is still taught in business schools today—it's practically the first lesson in corporate law. Students walk away with the understanding that their "fiduciary duty" is to maximize shareholder returns above all else.

But it doesn't have to be this way. There's nothing inevitable about corporations being heartless. For decades after Ford's time, some business leaders actually embraced the idea of being "stewards" of their communities. Think of the mid-twentieth-century factory towns where companies built housing, schools, and even hospitals for their workers. They understood that a thriving community created thriving companies.

So what would a modern fix look like? A few ideas:

- **Rewrite corporate law:** Congress or state legislatures could pass laws that expand fiduciary duty beyond just shareholders—requiring corporations to also consider employees, customers, and the community. This is sometimes called the *stakeholder model.*
- **B corporations and charters:** Today, companies can voluntarily register as "benefit corporations" that legally commit to balancing profit with social good. If it's voluntary now, why not make it the norm?
- **Tax incentives:** Reward companies that share profits with employees, raise wages, or invest in their local communities.
- **Worker representation:** In Germany, for example, workers sit on corporate boards. Imagine if American employees had a voice in how profits were shared.

Ultimately, undoing *Dodge v. Ford* isn't about a single courtroom reversal—it's about rewriting the social contract of business. Because a country where corporations are obligated to serve only shareholders is a country where workers and communities will always come last.

That precedent shows up everywhere—even in the way corporations handle their profits. Instead of rewarding workers or investing in innovation, they funnel billions into stock buybacks.

STOCK BUYBACKS: THE LEGALIZED WEALTH TRANSFER TO THE RICH

Here's something wild: For decades, stock buybacks were *illegal* in America. Why? Because they were considered blatant market manipulation. Companies weren't supposed to artificially pump up their own stock price—it was cheating.

But in the 1980s, Wall Street flexed its power. Regulators caved. And overnight, the cheat code became the rule book. What was once a crime turned into standard operating procedure.

Here's how it works.

Imagine a giant corporation just posted $10 billion in profits. They've got two choices for what to do with that cash:

1. **Invest in workers**—providing raises, better healthcare, maybe hiring more people.
2. **Buy back their own stock**—shrinking the number of shares so each one is instantly worth more, which sends the stock price soaring.

Guess which one they pick?

Buying back their own stock.

And it's not hard to see why. The people making the decision—the executives—are often paid in stock options. If the share price rises, their wealth explodes. A CEO's bonus might jump from $5 million to $50 million without inventing a new product, opening a new store, or giving a dime more to employees. It's like Wall Street alchemy: turn profits into personal jackpots.

But it's not just executive greed. The whole system pushes them this way:

- **Executive incentives:** Stock-based pay means leaders personally profit from buybacks.
- **Shareholder pressure:** Thanks to the *Dodge v. Ford* precedent, corporations are expected to maximize shareholder value. Skip buybacks and Wall Street punishes you.
- **Short-term obsession:** Hedge funds don't care about steady growth—they want instant pops in quarterly earnings. Buybacks deliver that fix.

Now, zoom out. The numbers are jaw-dropping.

- In **2022**, S&P 500 companies spent **$922 billion** on buybacks.[82]
- In **2023**, still a staggering **$795 billion.**[83]
- And by **2024**, a record **$942.5 billion**—nearly **$1 trillion** in a single year.[84]

Think about that. If even half of that cash had gone to wages? Every middle-class household in America could've felt it. That's the scale we're talking about.

Now, it's true—some middle-class Americans *do* benefit from buybacks. If you're invested in the stock market through a 401(k) or IRA, you might see your retirement account climb when stock prices rise. But here's the problem: That's not how most people experience economic growth. By investing directly in workers—raising wages and putting more money in the pockets of everyday Americans—that money flows back into the economy. Families spend it at the very companies they work for, driving demand, sales, and profits. And that, in turn, raises stock prices the natural way.

That's a win-win: Workers thrive, companies grow, and long-term investors benefit. But when corporations skip straight to buybacks, the gains get concentrated at the very top. Those who aren't invested—or who hold only a sliver of stock—get left behind.

Buybacks don't create anything new. No new jobs. No breakthrough technology. No community investment. Just numbers shifting on a screen while executives cash out.

Contrast that with a company like Costco—publicly traded but principled. Costco raises wages, provides healthcare, and still keeps investors happy. They prove it's not impossible. It's just a choice.

So how do we fix this? A few ideas:

- **Ban buybacks again.** We did it before—we can do it again.
- **Reward real investment.** Give tax credits to companies that raise wages, build innovation, or share ownership with workers.
- **Shift the culture.** Remind corporate America that real value comes from people, not Wall Street fireworks.

Because here's the truth: Stock buybacks aren't just a financial trick. They're a choice. And every time a company chooses them, they're saying out loud: *We'd rather make the rich richer than build a stronger middle class.*

And for whatever's left? The trick is to hide it offshore. Enter shell companies and tax havens.

SHELL COMPANIES: THE ULTIMATE BILLIONAIRE TAX LOOPHOLE

When you hear "the Cayman Islands," you probably think of turquoise water, yachts, and piña coladas under the sun. And yes, it's paradise—but not just for vacationers. It's also a tax paradise, home to tens of thousands of shell companies. In fact, the Cayman Islands has more registered companies than actual people.[85] For billionaires and big corporations, those white-sand beaches are less about cocktails and more about hiding money.

Picture this: MegaCorp earns $50 billion in revenue. After paying employees, covering expenses, and everything else, they're left with $10 billion in profit.

Now, under US law, corporate profits are taxed (currently) at 21 percent. So on that $10 billion, MegaCorp should be writing a check for about $2.1 billion in taxes.

Except . . . they don't.

Instead of reporting the full $10 billion profit in the US, MegaCorp sets up a shell company—let's call it ParadiseInc—in a tax haven like the Cayman Islands. On paper, that ParadiseInc "owns" a patent, trademark, or brand license. Then, they "pay" that shell company $4 billion in royalties or consulting fees. Nothing is really exchanged—it's just money being shifted from one pocket to another. But on paper? MegaCorp's US profits have magically shrunk to $6 billion.

Now their tax bill isn't $2.1 billion. It's $1.26 billion. Just like that, they've shaved *$840 million* off their taxes—money that could've funded schools, hospitals, or infrastructure. Instead, it's sitting in the Caribbean far from the communities that helped generate it.

And it doesn't stop there. If MegaCorp wants to use that money, ParadiseInc can lend it back to the US parent. MegaCorp US pays interest back to its Cayman subsidiary. MegaCorp US then can deduct that *interest* as a business expense, lowering US taxable profit even more.

And here's the bigger picture: When you line this up next to stock buybacks, you start to see the pattern. The money is there—trillions of dollars in profits. It's just not going to workers, or communities, or the middle class. Instead, it's shuffled into shell companies or funneled back into Wall Street fireworks.

Every time a company makes these choices, they're telling us exactly who the system was built to serve.

Spoiler: It isn't us.

WHAT'S THE NEXT MOVE?

So now that we've seen how the system is tilted—and how policies like buybacks, lobbying, and shell companies widen the gap—the natural question is: *What do we do about it?*

On paper, the simplest fix would be to raise the top federal income tax rate. And yes, in theory, boosting it from 37 percent to 45 percent or 50 percent would raise another $100–$150 billion a year. But unfortunately, it wouldn't move the needle enough to change the game. And worse, it might hit doctors, lawyers, and small-business owners harder than it hits billionaires, because billionaires don't really "earn" in salaries the way the rest of us do. They live off assets. So hiking income taxes misses the target.

That's why some lawmakers have floated more creative approaches—ways to tax *wealth itself,* rather than just income.

TAXING UNREALIZED GAINS

Imagine a billionaire whose stock rockets upward, adding $40 billion to her net worth in a single year. On paper, she's richer than ever. But unless she sells, she pays zero taxes on that $40 billion. A tax on unrealized gains would change that, forcing her to contribute something even without a sale.

Sounds fair. But here's the snag: Asset values swing daily. Do we tax someone at the peak, only for the value to crash the next year? How do we handle illiquid assets like art or private companies? It's messy. Economists like the idea in theory, but in practice it's complicated to implement and even harder to enforce.

A WEALTH TAX

This idea is cleaner. Instead of taxing "paper gains," you tax total net worth above a high threshold—say, $50 million. A 2 percent wealth tax on someone worth $10 billion would mean a $200 million bill every year, regardless of whether they sell a single share of stock.

Some politicians have championed this approach, pointing out that even a small annual tax on extreme wealth could raise $200–$300 billion a year—roughly $2–$3 trillion over a decade.[86] And unlike income taxes, which miss most of the ultrarich, this targets the true source of inequality: the massive stockpiles of assets concentrated at the very top.

But it comes with big challenges. How do you fairly value assets that aren't publicly traded? How do you close loopholes when billionaires can hire the smartest tax lawyers on Earth? And does the IRS even have the manpower to enforce it? Many experts argue it's more practical than taxing unrealized gains—but still far from a silver bullet.[87]

And there's a bigger issue. Even if we raised the federal income tax, added a tax on unrealized gains, or passed a wealth tax, it all feels like patchwork. Even if those policies raised $500 billion more a year, the US, in recent years, still spent around $6 to $7 trillion annually funded by roughly $5 trillion in tax revenue and another $1–$2 trillion in deficit spending.[88] Sure, it might shrink the deficit—but does it actually change the lives of everyday workers right now?

That's the problem. Taxing unrealized gains or implementing a wealth tax may sound bold, but they risk feeling like confiscation, and they'd spark endless battles over valuation and enforcement. I don't want a system that pits billionaires against everyone else. I want one where billionaires, corporations, and everyday Americans can thrive together.

Because the truth is, America doesn't lack money. We don't lack productivity. We don't lack resources. What we lack is a system that puts people first.

I really think the only lasting solution is this: ban Super PACs, curb stock buybacks, and—most importantly—change the business model of "profits over people" into "people first."

What does "people first" look like? It looks like *higher wages*. It looks like profit sharing and employee ownership. It looks like corporations finally realizing that when workers thrive, businesses thrive. Imagine if the energy and creativity of 175 million working Americans were unleashed—not just surviving paycheck to paycheck, but investing, saving, and building wealth for their families.

It's smart economics. When we all have more money, we spend it. We buy homes, cars, groceries, childcare. We invest in the stock market and retirement accounts. That spending and investing flows right back into the economy, fueling the very companies paying them in the first place. Everyone wins.

We've tried the trickle-down model for decades, and it's failed. The wealth didn't trickle—it pooled at the top. So instead of endlessly patching a broken system—raising this tax here or inventing a new one there—what if we started asking a different question: What would a tax system look like if it were designed to help working Americans thrive first, not just manage inequality after the fact?

MY NEW TAX PROPOSAL

I believe the only realistic way to save the middle class—and give Americans a real shot at thriving again—is to eliminate payroll taxes entirely and remove federal income taxes on the first $100,000 of W-2 income.

Because if we're honest about the math, there are only two ways the American Dream becomes attainable again: Either the cost of living—housing, childcare, college, healthcare, utilities—comes down dramatically, or wages rise by about 50 percent.

A sudden drop in prices would likely require a major economic crash, which would be devastating and create far more problems than it solves. And while higher wages across the board would be the healthier outcome in theory, it's hard to believe that millions of businesses—large and small—are suddenly going to wake up one morning and voluntarily raise pay by 50 percent. That just isn't realistic.

Could the government step in and mandate a "living wage"? Possibly. But that approach comes with its own set of complications, loopholes, and unintended consequences. So instead of forcing wages up or hoping prices magically come down, there's a cleaner solution: Let people keep more of the money they already earn.

This idea isn't perfect. No large reform ever is. But I believe it's fair, realistic, and worth discussing. So imagine this: Tomorrow, I'm in charge for one day. I announce that the federal tax system as we know it is gone.

The IRS's tens of thousands of pages of rules and regulations? Gone. The loopholes, write-offs, and tax games? Gone.

In their place, we implement **four simple taxes** that raise roughly the same revenue as today—but finally allow the middle class to breathe.

STEP 1: NO FEDERAL TAX ON THE FIRST $100,000 OF W-2 INCOME

Every W-2 employee pays zero federal income tax on their first $100,000 of earnings.

That means no federal withholding. No FICA. No April panic. For tens of millions of Americans, federal taxes simply disappear. When you get your paycheck, it's your paycheck. (Maybe minus state taxes—but federally, it's yours.)

That alone would instantly put thousands of dollars back into people's pockets and improve quality of life in a way we haven't seen in generations. (Anyone who's ever earned $5,000 a month and only taken home $4,200 knows that feeling—it feels like something was taken from you before you even had a chance to hold it.)

But if we're going to do this, we also have to be honest about the math: The federal government still needs to raise about $5 trillion a year to function. Here's how that happens.

STEP 2: A FLAT 30 PERCENT TAX ON W-2 INCOME ABOVE $100,000

For income above $100,000, every W-2 employee pays a simple flat tax of 30 percent.

So if you earn $200,000:

- You pay zero tax on the first $100,000;
- You pay 30 percent on the second $100,000;
- Your total federal tax bill is $30,000.

Under today's system, that same worker would likely pay closer to $40–$45K between federal income tax and payroll taxes. So this system helps middle- and upper-middle-class workers too.

And yes, that means a CEO earning $20 million would write a $6 million check.

Some people will say, "That's not enough." But the goal here isn't punishment—it's fairness, simplicity, and sustainability. This step alone would raise roughly $1 trillion in federal revenue.

STEP 3 (THE CONTROVERSIAL ONE): A 5 PERCENT GROSS-REVENUE TAX ON ALL BUSINESSES

This is the part people usually push back on, so let's walk through it. Every business in America—large or small—pays a 5 percent tax on gross revenue. No write-offs. No deductions. No loopholes. No armies of accountants. If you sell something, 5 percent goes to the government. That's it.

Amazon does $1 trillion in sales? They pay $50 billion. A landscaping company earns $1 million? They pay $50,000. A freelancer or content creator earns $200,000? They pay $10,000.

Clean. Simple. Transparent.

Right now, businesses spend billions gaming the tax code—hiring accountants, lawyers, and lobbyists to legally avoid paying what they owe. Under this system, all of that disappears. There's no advantage to hiding income, no benefit to complexity. You earn money, you pay 5 percent. Done.

Many people will ask, "But what about small businesses?" This is the first—and fairest—concern. Some small businesses operate on thin margins. Under this system, many would need to raise prices by 5 to 10 percent to stay whole. But here's the trade-off: Their customers—millions of them—are now keeping thousands more dollars of their own money every year because they're no longer paying payroll taxes or federal income tax on their first $100,000.

So if dinner for two goes from $50 to $55, but you're no longer losing nearly 20 percent of your paycheck to taxes, most people would gladly make that trade. A couch that used to cost $2,000 might now cost $2,100 or $2,200. A flat-screen TV might go from $200 to $220. Prices go up slightly—but disposable income goes up a lot.

This system also removes a massive burden from corporations. No payroll taxes. No corporate income taxes. No tax strategists. No international shell games. If a company does $1 billion in sales, they know exactly what they owe: $50 million. That predictability matters. It makes planning easier, investment safer, and compliance cheaper.

And here's the part we don't talk about enough: This model rewards growth, not manipulation. Under today's system, companies often grow by squeezing wages, cutting corners, or avoiding taxes. Under this system, growth means something different. The more sales a company generates, the more tax revenue it contributes—without punishing labor or innovation.

The bigger shift is that this creates a trickle-up economy, and this is where the model flips. When tens of millions of Americans suddenly keep more of their paycheck, they don't stash it offshore. They spend it. They invest it. They start businesses. They buy homes.

And where does that money go? Right back into the companies selling goods and services. More spending leads to more sales. More sales lead to more tax revenue. More tax revenue funds the government—without crushing workers.

Right now, when we hear that corporations are posting record profits and record growth, it often feels disconnected from our own lives—like someone else is winning a game we're not even allowed to play. But under this system, that changes.

When America's biggest companies grow, we all participate in that success. Every dollar they earn sends five cents directly back into the system that supports the country. Their growth helps fund our schools, our infrastructure, and our government—without squeezing workers or hiding behind loopholes.

Instead of feeling left out, we feel invested.

I'd *want* to spend money at those companies, knowing part of every purchase is going back to the people. I'd *want* to invest in them, knowing that their success directly strengthens the country we all share. Growth stops feeling like something that happens *to* us, and starts feeling like something we're part of.

That's how you heal the divide—not by tearing success down, but by finally letting everyone share in it. This single tax would generate roughly $2.5 trillion in revenue while simplifying the system, reducing corruption, and aligning incentives in a way that finally makes sense.

STEP 4: A 5 PERCENT FEDERAL CONSUMPTION TAX—WITH PROTECTION FOR LOW EARNERS

The next piece of the puzzle is a 5 percent federal consumption tax on goods and services—similar to a state sales tax most Americans are already familiar with. This tax applies at the point of purchase, not the paycheck. If you buy something, you contribute a small amount. If you don't, you don't. Simple.

On its own, a consumption tax can feel regressive. Lower-income households tend to spend a larger share of what they earn, so price increases hit them harder. That concern is real—and it's exactly why this tax doesn't exist in isolation. By the time we get here, tens of millions of Americans are already keeping far more of their income because they're no longer paying payroll taxes or federal income tax on their first $100,000. For most households, that gain alone more than offsets a modest increase at the register.

And we're going to take it one step further: Anyone earning $50,000 or less—whether it comes from wages, Social Security, disability benefits, or a pension—would receive a $3,000 annual UBI payment. No means-testing. No conditions. No paperwork or hoops to jump through. Just a simple, once-a-year payment designed to ensure that all Americans come out ahead under this system.

Here's what that looks like in real life: Take someone earning $20,000 a year today. Under the current system, they lose about 7.65 percent of their paycheck to payroll taxes—roughly $1,500 a year—and many pay little to no federal income tax after deductions and credits. Under this new system:

- They keep that entire $1,500 by eliminating payroll taxes;
- They pay no federal income tax;
- They receive an additional $3,000 UBI payment.

That's an immediate gain of roughly $4,500 a year.

Even if that person spends their entire $20,000 and pays a 5 percent consumption tax—about $1,000—they still come out ahead. And even in a worst-case scenario where businesses pass the full 5 percent gross-revenue tax through into prices (another roughly $1,000 on $20,000 of spending), they're still more than $2,000 ahead. For the vast majority of Americans, this system results in a net gain, not just breaking even. And because existing programs like SNAP, housing assistance, and Medicaid aren't taken away, this added income becomes real breathing room—money that can go toward stability, emergencies, or finally getting ahead.

A consumption tax does something income taxes don't: It taxes what you use, not what you earn. People who consume more—especially on discretionary or luxury spending—naturally contribute more. People who consume less aren't punished simply for working or trying to survive.

It also captures revenue from places the current system struggles to reach:

- Tourists
- High spenders who minimize taxable income
- Cash-heavy transactions

Because the rate is low and broad, there's little incentive to avoid it—and very little room for games. This step would raise close to $1 trillion in revenue while keeping the system transparent, predictable, and easy to understand.

Most importantly, this part of the system is scalable. As productivity increases, technology advances, and the economy grows, the benefits can grow too. That $3,000 payment can increase and eventually so could the income limit. Prosperity doesn't get trapped at the top—it circulates. Instead of asking, *"How do we take more?"* the system starts asking, *"How do we share growth better?"* That's the difference between a tax code designed to get by—and one designed to help people thrive.

STEP 5: CAPITAL GAINS—KEPT AS-IS

The final piece of this system is capital gains taxes—exactly as they are today. No overhaul. No new brackets. No dramatic increases. Investment income continues to be taxed the same way it is now—because it already plays an important role in funding the government.

Capital gains are taxes paid on profits from assets—things you own, not wages you earn. When someone sells a stock, a business, or a piece of real estate for more than they paid for it, the profit is taxed as a capital gain. Unlike wages, capital gains are only taxed when the asset is sold.

The system is already tiered. Most Americans pay zero or 15 percent on capital gains, depending on their income. Only the highest earners pay the top 20 percent rate (plus the existing investment surtax). In other words, this tax primarily applies to people who already have assets—not people living paycheck to paycheck.

In recent years, capital gains taxes have generated roughly $200–$300 billion annually, though the exact number rises and falls with the markets.[89] In strong years, it's higher. In weaker years, it's lower. That volatility is precisely why capital gains work best as a supporting pillar, not the backbone of the system. And that's exactly how this plan treats them. We don't punish investing. We don't discourage risk-taking. We simply keep capital gains in place so that when markets boom and assets appreciate, a portion of that upside flows back into the country that made that growth possible. Work is no longer overtaxed. Consumption contributes fairly. Businesses fund the system when they grow. And capital participates—without being singled out or shielded.

That balance matters.

HERE'S WHAT IT LOOKS LIKE WHEN YOU PUT IT ALL TOGETHER

To replace the roughly $5 trillion the federal government currently collects each year, this system relies on four main revenue streams:

- A 30 percent flat tax on individual income above $100,000, which would raise about $1 trillion
- A 5 percent gross-revenue tax on all businesses, which would raise roughly $2.5 trillion
- A 5 percent federal consumption tax, generating about $1 trillion
- Capital gains taxes in a strong market year, contributing around $300 billion

Together, that totals roughly $4.8 trillion in annual revenue.

From that, we fund the $3,000 UBI for Americans earning $50,000 or less, which costs about $300 billion per year—bringing net revenue to around $4.5 trillion.

That's not a perfect match for today's federal budget. But it's close enough to show what's possible—especially when you factor in that a simpler system would reduce tax avoidance, and that long-term economic growth and smarter government spending could close the remaining gap.

This isn't a finished blueprint. It's a starting point, a way to rethink how we fund government in a world where the old rules no longer work.

THIS NEW SYSTEM VS. THE CURRENT SYSTEM

One system is simple, transparent, and rewards work. The other is bloated, confusing, and quietly punishes the people who keep the country running.

One system says, "If you work, you should be able to live." The other says, "Figure it out—or fall behind."

We've been conditioned to believe that changing the rules is too complicated—while accepting a system that clearly isn't working for most people. That's the real absurdity. So no, this isn't about me having all the answers. It's about finally asking the right question: If we were designing the American tax system from scratch today—knowing what we know now—would we ever choose the one we're living under? I don't think we would. And I think, deep down, most Americans know it too.

The next chapter of the American story has to be about building from the middle out: wages tied to productivity, corporations rewarded for reinvesting in people, and a cultural shift where prosperity is shared, not hoarded.

If we get that right, the American Dream isn't dead. It's just waiting to be reclaimed.

And while fixing the system will take time, here's the empowering truth: You don't have to wait for Washington or Wall Street to change. In the final chapter, "The New American Dream," we'll talk about what you can do right now—practical, step-by-step moves to take your finances into your own hands, build wealth, and start seeing results immediately.

Chapter 13

THE NEW AMERICAN DREAM

At the core, the American Dream looks different for each of us— but we all share one thing in common: We don't want to feel like we're here just to work, grabbing slivers of life whenever we can.

No one dreams of making $50,000 a year for ten years, earning $500,000 total—only to wake up and realize they have nothing to show for it. That's the treadmill most people are stuck on: running hard, staying in place.

Everywhere we turn, consumerism and materialism whisper in our ear: Buy more, upgrade, lease, finance, subscribe. And when we finally stop and look at the numbers, we ask ourselves: *Why isn't life easier if the US has the largest economy in the world?* Sure, most of us have air-conditioning, streaming services, and a supercomputer in our pocket. But the basics—housing, healthcare, childcare, education—are harder than ever to afford.

And so, more and more people are opting out. Selling everything to move across the country, or even across the world, just for the chance at a slower pace, a little freedom, and the space to do what they love. Deep down, that's what we all want: for our work to actually move our lives forward, and for our time to be spent with the people who matter most.

For some, that dream means work-life balance. For others, it's the stability of a steady nine-to-five. And for others, it's the chance to climb higher, earn more, and enjoy the luxuries of life. Personally, I've always been driven to build, to earn, and to experience more—but it took me years to learn how to balance ambition with freedom.

And here's the truth: The system isn't designed to make that balance easy. We've spent this book pulling back the curtain on policies, loopholes, and corporate greed that tilt the playing field so far in favor of the ultrawealthy that ordinary people feel like they're sprinting uphill just to stay in place.

But this is the moment that matters: *What do we do about it?*

This is the part no one can take from us. Not Wall Street, not Washington, not billionaires hiding their money offshore. They may control the rules of the system, but we control how we play the game.

And that's what this chapter is all about: rewriting the rules for ourselves. Not waiting for a politician to save us. Not resigning ourselves to a life of debt and struggle. But choosing a new path—one that gives us back our time, our freedom, and our sense of possibility.

So at this point, we have three choices.

OPTION 1: KEEP PLAYING THE OLD GAME

This is the default path—the one most people fall into without even realizing it. It's the path of grinding fifty to sixty hours a week, doing everything "right," and still ending up exhausted and stuck. You eat at home, cut coupons, work harder, and hope it eventually adds up to security. But here's the truth: For most people today, this path doesn't lead to freedom. It leads to burnout.

Why? Because under this model, you're running on a treadmill that never slows down. Every time you make progress, the incline cranks higher. Rent goes up. Groceries cost more. Interest payments eat away at your paycheck. You're sweating, you're hustling, but you're not actually moving forward.

And if we're being brutally honest? That's exactly where the system wants you—tired, too busy, too distracted to question why you're not getting ahead.

Now, let's be fair. The old game did work for previous generations. Wages were in line with the cost of living. National debt was lower. Personal debt was manageable. Life wasn't carved up into subscriptions and hidden fees. Back then, discipline alone—saving diligently, buying a modest home, driving one car for twenty years—could eventually get you to financial freedom.

But today? Discipline isn't enough. In a world this expensive, we need more than discipline—we need strategy.

That doesn't mean the old path is completely dead. For some, especially higher earners who live well within their means, it can still work. My wife and I are proof. After years of being crushed by debt and trapped by lifestyle inflation, we finally broke free by redefining what success meant for us. Together, we make over $200,000 a year—but here's the key: We chose a modest home, modest cars, and a lifestyle that only requires about $100,000.

The result? Freedom. We could stretch ourselves into a bigger house or flashier cars, but that would only buy us a fancier version of the same trap. Instead, we bought freedom: the ability to make decisions based on what's best for our lives, not our lifestyle. And that shift—understanding that freedom, not stuff, is the real goal—has made us feel wealthier than ever.

OPTION 2: WAIT FOR A HERO (WHO'S STUCK IN TRAFFIC)

The second path is tempting. It's the path of waiting for politicians and our system to change. Waiting for a leader to ride in on a white horse and "fix" what's broken. After all, politicians promise us relief every election cycle. Student-debt forgiveness, cheaper healthcare, more affordable housing—we've all heard the speeches. And for a moment, it feels like maybe, just maybe, this time they'll actually deliver.

But systemic change moves glacially slow. And the people we're counting on to save us? More often than not, they're entangled in the very system we're hoping they'll dismantle. For every bill that promises to help the middle class, there's a lobbyist waiting with a check to water it down. For every campaign ad promising "real change," there's a billionaire donor whispering in the candidate's ear about how far that change should actually go.

Waiting for a hero often means waiting forever. And in the meantime, the inflation, debt, and taxes keep eroding our financial foundation.

That doesn't mean fighting for change isn't important—it is. March, protest, vote, speak up. Every step matters. But if there's one thing history has taught us, it's this: Real change is slow, messy, and always comes with pushback. If you hang your entire future on Washington suddenly coming to its senses, you'll be waiting a long time.

That's why the real power of this option isn't choosing it—it's blending it. Fight for change. Demand better policies. Hold leaders accountable. But don't make the mistake of outsourcing your entire financial future to someone else's timeline. Because the truth is, the cavalry isn't coming fast enough. And in the meantime, you've got moves you can make on your own.

OPTION 3: REWRITE THE RULES TO WORK FOR YOU

This option is the one I believe our generation is really searching for. It's the path of ownership—not just of houses or cars, but of our time, our freedom, and our future. It's where we stop following someone else's outdated road map and start designing our own.

Choosing this path doesn't mean ignoring the fight for bigger change. It means refusing to sit on the sidelines while it happens. It's about building your own freedom brick by brick, paycheck by paycheck, choice by choice.

And it's about redefining success itself. For decades, the milestones were fixed: Go to school, graduate college, get a job, climb the ladder at the same company for forty years, get married, have kids, buy a house. That path still works for some, and there's nothing wrong with it. But today, it should be one *option*—not the default. Our generation is writing a different script: one where freedom of time, flexibility, and the ability to choose work we actually love matter just as much as traditional milestones.

And here's the best part: This dream is possible. It doesn't require waiting for Washington. It doesn't require being born rich. It requires being intentional—playing the game on your own terms and investing in your own freedom.

Because this isn't just about higher costs of living—it's about an entirely different world. Millennials especially know this firsthand: We had one foot in the past and one in the future. We grew up in a world of landlines, malls, and stable careers—and then watched it transform into a world of iPhones, AI, gig work, and social media jobs that didn't even exist a decade ago. The pace of change has only accelerated, and it's not slowing down.

Which brings us to my next point: The future is changing so quickly that clinging to the old American Dream just doesn't make sense anymore. The real question isn't "How do I follow the same script that previous generations did?" but rather "How do I stay flexible enough to thrive in a world that will look completely different every five years?"

A WORLD THAT'S CHANGING FAST

Here's a truth we can't ignore: We're living in unprecedented times.

What are the odds that someone graduating college in 2025 will get hired at one company and stay until retirement? Practically zero.

Why? Because technology—especially AI—is rewriting the rules of work in real time. Entire industries are being disrupted, and the pace is only accelerating. The reality is that most of us will reinvent ourselves every five to ten years. That might mean changing industries, changing careers, or even changing cities. Renting instead of owning might become the default—because flexibility is the new wealth.

And we need to give ourselves some credit here. We're the first generation living through a period where change is exponential, not linear. Back in the day, progress was slow. My high school experience looked almost identical to my parents'. Culture shifted at a crawl. Planning for the future was predictable.

But for us? In just twenty years, malls went from the center of social life to ghost towns. Netflix went from mailing DVDs to dominating our free time. Smartphones went from novelty gadgets to permanent extensions of our hands. Social media—something that didn't even exist when many of us graduated high school—has now created entire new industries. I mean, my own career as a content creator wasn't even a possibility when I was a teenager. Today, it's not only real—it's global.

So, what will exist in the next ten years? The next thirty? None of us can fully picture it. But that doesn't mean we should freeze up or panic. It just means the old road map doesn't work anymore for most people.

The way forward isn't trying to predict the future—it's building the *flexibility to pivot when it changes*. And that comes down to three things:

1. **Getting rid of debt** (so you're not chained to yesterday's choices)
2. **Freeing up your paycheck** (so you have the breathing room to take calculated risks)
3. **Investing in assets and yourself** (so your money and your skills keep growing, no matter what jobs or industries rise and fall)

That's the playbook for living in a world that refuses to sit still.

WHAT'S REALLY DRAINING YOUR MONEY

Now before we can rebuild, we first need to understand what's been quietly draining our money all along. That's where the leaky bucket comes in. Your income is water pouring into a bucket—but the bucket isn't watertight. It has leaks. Unless you manage these leaks, no matter how much water you pour in, the bucket never seems to fill.

These leaks come in the forms of **inflation, interest,** and **taxation.**

INFLATION: THE SLOW DRIP

This is the quiet leak at the bottom. It doesn't gush—it drips, day after day, year after year, slowly draining your money until one day you realize how much is gone. On average, inflation erodes about 3 percent of your money every year. That doesn't sound catastrophic—until you zoom out.

Imagine pouring $100 into your bucket. By the end of the year, the small drip has left you with the buying power of $97. Ten years later, that same $100 holds the value of only $74. You didn't spend a dime—but the bucket leaked anyway.

Now this particular hole in the bucket cannot be patched. It exists at the bottom of everyone's bucket. It doesn't matter your income level.

So how do you fight back? You can't plug the leak—inflation is baked into the system. But you can outpace it by pouring water in faster than it drips out, by putting your money into assets that grow faster than inflation: stocks, real estate, or any investment that historically beats it.

That same $100 invested in the stock market at an 8 percent return still loses 3 percent to the drip, but you end the year at $105—stronger than where you started.

Here are a few practical options:

- Open a Roth IRA (if you qualify based on income) or a brokerage account (no income limits). Reputable companies include Vanguard, Fidelity, and Charles Schwab.
- Pick a broad, low-cost index fund—like VOO (S&P 500) or VTI (total stock market).
- Set up automatic contributions—even $50 or $100 a month adds up. The key is consistency, not timing the market.

That's it. No day-trading. No obsessing over stock tips. Just own a piece of the entire economy and let time do the heavy lifting. This way you can have those investments filling up your bucket.

Then, there's another way to slow the drip: **high-yield savings accounts (HYSAs).**

These are perfect for your emergency fund because they're safe, liquid, and often earn 3–5 percent interest. A few popular options include:

- Ally Bank
- Marcus by Goldman Sachs
- Capital One 360 Performance Savings
- American Express High-Yield Savings

With rates like these, your $100 isn't shrinking. If inflation runs at 3 percent and your HYSA earns 3–4 percent, you're at least breaking even instead of falling behind.

The takeaway? Leaving money in cash or a basic savings account is like letting the drip run unchecked—a guaranteed slow drain.

INTEREST: THE SIDE HOLES

This leak is sneakier. It doesn't drain your money all at once—it tempts you first. "You deserve that car. Take the trip. Buy now, pay later." You swipe your card, sign the loan, and suddenly your bucket has extra holes punched in the sides.

Here's how the interest drains you:

- A used car at 10 percent interest = hundreds of dollars leaking out every month.
- Student loans at 8 percent = another steady stream.
- A mortgage at 7 percent = even more gone. (Though this one could be worth it.)
- Credit cards at 20–29 percent? That's not just a leak—that's a flood.

Now, not all interest is bad if you plan accordingly. Some leaks may cost you in the short term but actually help you fill your bucket faster in the long run.

Take student loans as an example. Yes, they can spill a lot of water out the side of your bucket, but if paying them back helps you earn a degree that unlocks a higher-paying career, then the temporary leak might be worth it. In that case, the income you gain later more than makes up for the water you lost early on.

The same goes for a mortgage. At first, the interest is brutal—you're losing thousands of dollars a year. But if you make extra principal payments to shrink the leak faster, and your home appreciates over time (as US homes historically have, around 4 percent annually), then the cost of the leak may be offset by the value your home is gaining.

This is where math and discipline matter. Each percentage point of interest is water you can't keep in the bucket—money you can't invest, money that isn't compounding for your future. Wealthy people understand this. They borrow at 4 percent only if they're confident they can earn 10 percent. They use debt as a tool.

Most people, however, fall into the trap of **bad debt**—credit cards and car loans. Unlike a home, a car loses value the second you drive it off the lot. If you keep buying new cars every few years, you're not only dealing with the interest leak, you're also stuck with a liability that's depreciating at the same time. That's a double drain.

The more debt you carry, the more holes in your bucket—and the harder it becomes to ever fill it.

TAXES: THE BIGGEST LEAK

Taxes are one of the largest leaks in your financial bucket. Some are unavoidable—property taxes, sales tax, the yearly bill just to keep your car on the road. Others, though, can be managed with the right strategy.

If you're a W-2 employee, 20–30 percent of your paycheck disappears before it even reaches your account. Then more leaks show up at the gas pump, the grocery store, and on that annual property tax statement. It's constant. It's everywhere.

Wealthy people know this is their single biggest expense, so they treat it differently. They own businesses (where write-offs are plentiful), they invest in real estate (with tax breaks baked in), and they borrow against assets instead of selling them (avoiding taxable "income").

Most of us weren't taught any of this in high school. We were told: Work hard, pay your fair share, and hope for the best. But without some kind of strategy, you're just standing by while your bucket slowly drains.

Now, if you're a W-2 employee, you don't have as many levers as a business owner or investor—but you do have options:

1. **Start a side hustle.** Even small gigs can open the door to deductions: part of your phone bill, mileage, internet, and more.

2. **Explore real estate.** Rental properties allow deductions on mortgage interest, property taxes, maintenance, and depreciation.
3. **Use retirement accounts strategically.** A traditional IRA or 401(k) lowers taxable income today; a Roth IRA grows tax free for the future.

None of these are silver bullets, and not everyone can use them all. But the point is this: You don't have to accept every leak in your bucket. With education and intention, you can legally and ethically reduce how much water seeps out.

Start small:

- Read books.
- Listen to podcasts.
- Take online courses.
- Network with people in the field.

The more you learn, the better equipped you'll be to keep more water in your bucket. Because while taxes are inevitable, you don't have to lose as much as you are now.

PUTTING IT TOGETHER: A $70,000 REALITY CHECK

At this point, you can see the problem: It's not just one leak holding us back—it's all of them. Inflation drips from the bottom. Interest gushes from the sides. Taxes punch new holes straight through the bucket.

Individually, each feels manageable. But together, the damage is staggering. And most people don't realize how much is draining until they step back and do the math.

To understand this, let's meet Jason. Jason is twenty-nine, works full time, and earns $70,000 a year. On paper, that looks solid—above the US median. But let's see what happens when the leaks hit his bucket.

STEP 1: TAXES (THE BIGGEST LEAK)

Before Jason can pay a single bill, about $14,000 drains away through federal income tax, Social Security, and Medicare. Nearly $1,200 a month is gone before groceries, rent, or gas. His $70,000 is really closer to $56,000 take home.

STEP 2: THE CAR LOAN (SIDE HOLE #1)

Jason financed a $30,000 car at 10 percent interest. His monthly payment is $650, but about $250 of that is just interest. That's $3,000 a year leaking away.

STEP 3: STUDENT LOANS (SIDE HOLE #2)

He owes $25,000 at 8 percent interest, costing about $250 a month. Of that, $167 is interest—another $2,000 a year gone.

STEP 4: CREDIT CARDS (THE BIGGEST SIDE HOLE)

Jason carries a $5,000 balance on a card at 20 percent interest. His minimum payment is $150, but $83 of that is interest. That's $1,000 gone over the year, and the balance barely shrinks.

STEP 5: INFLATION (THE DRIP)

Jason does the "responsible" thing and saves $300 a month in a standard account—$3,600 a year. But with 3 percent inflation, the drip drains away $108 in value. Over ten years, his $36,000 would be worth closer to $28,000 in today's dollars.

ADD IT ALL UP FOR THE YEAR

- Taxes: $14,000
- Car loan interest: $3,000
- Student loan interest: $2,000
- Credit card interest: $1,000
- Inflation on savings: $108

That's more than *$20,000 drained from Jason's bucket every year.*

And here's the thing—Jason doesn't feel broke. He has a decent salary, a car, a place to live. But no matter how hard he works, his bucket never fills. His paycheck isn't building wealth—it's leaking away.

That's the quiet trap most of us are in. We're not failing because we're lazy or irresponsible. We're failing because the system is designed to siphon off our money before we ever get the chance to build freedom with it.

But, fortunately, the leaks can be managed. You can fight back. By budgeting with purpose, making intentional sacrifices, and increasing your income the right way, you can flip the script. Instead of feeding the termites, you can finally start feeding your future.

So if we want to escape the cycle of debt, burnout, and disappointment, we need to redefine the rules and build a playbook that works for our reality.

Here's how.

STEP 1: BUDGET WITH PURPOSE

Forget the idea that budgeting means punishing yourself. Forget cutting every joy out of your life. Budgeting isn't about deprivation—it's about direction. It's about pointing your money toward the life you actually want instead of letting it leak into things that don't matter.

That means ignoring the "milestones" society still tries to guilt us into:

- Still living at home to save money? That's not lazy—that's smart.
- Driving a ten-year-old car instead of leasing a shiny new one? That's financially savvy.
- Choosing concerts, trips, or time with friends over material status symbols? That's the new American Dream in action.

A budget says: *I'm not living to impress anyone else. I'm living for freedom.*

Ask yourself:

- What actually improves my life? (Travel? Music? Great food?)
- What's just noise? (Do I really need eight streaming services?)

When you see it this way, your budget stops being a prison and becomes your road map.

STEP 2: MAKE INTENTIONAL SACRIFICES

If you're drowning in debt or way behind on savings, skipping Starbucks won't save you. Small cuts won't move the needle. You need bold, intentional sacrifices—short-term pain for long-term freedom.

- **Get a roommate.** Sharing rent for just one year could save you $10,000—enough to wipe out credit card debt or seed an investment account.
- **Pick up extra work.** A second job that brings in $1,000/month means $12,000 in a single year. That could erase a student loan balance.
- **Relocate temporarily.** Moving even an hour outside a major city could slash rent by hundreds every month. Do that for two years, and you could save enough for a down payment.

Remember that these aren't forever decisions. You're not signing up for a lifetime of roommates or doubles at a second job. You're making strategic sacrifices now so you can buy your freedom later.

And the most important part? *Make it count.* If you're serving tables on weekends and bringing in an extra $2,000 a month, don't let that money get lost in lifestyle creep. Every dollar should be directed toward a goal that matters—paying off debt, building savings, or investing.

For example:

- If you have $20,000 in debt and commit all $2,000/month from your side job to it, you'll be debt free in ten months.
- That's not just a clean slate—it's also eliminating a $300 monthly payment. That's $300 every single month you've now freed up to invest, save, or actually enjoy.

Think of every dollar you free up as a worker. If you waste it, that worker stays unemployed. But if you send it out to fight for your future—in debt payoff or investing—it comes back with reinforcements. That's how freedom is built.

STEP 3: INCREASE YOUR INCOME (THE GAME CHANGER)

Here's the most important truth in personal finance: You can only cut so much, but your earning potential is limitless.

Yes, saving matters. But you'll never save your way to wealth. The fastest path to financial freedom is growing your income—and then using that extra money wisely.

- **Switch jobs strategically.** If you're making $3,200/month waiting tables at Applebee's, maybe you could make $4,500 at a high-end steakhouse. Same hours. Bigger tips.
- **Learn a high-income skill.** Sales, real estate, digital marketing, AI—these don't require a degree, but they can double your income in a few years.

- **Start a side hustle.** Freelance design, tutoring, content creation, e-commerce. Every extra dollar you bring in is another dollar you can put to work.

But here's the golden rule: *Don't inflate your lifestyle just because your income goes up*. That's the trap.

Most people (my wife and I included, years ago) get a raise and immediately upgrade: a nicer car, a bigger apartment, fancier dinners. At first it feels great. But the dopamine rush fades, and all you're left with are higher bills. Suddenly, you're still living paycheck to paycheck—just in a nicer place.

The real power comes when you resist that urge. Instead, funnel every raise, every promotion, every side hustle dollar into assets: paying down debt, investing in index funds, or saving for real estate. Because the moment your money starts making money without you working? That's the moment you win the game.

And here's the hidden benefit: When you build a cushion—a healthy savings account and growing investments—you buy yourself peace of mind. The first thought in the morning isn't *How am I going to pay my bills?* but: *What opportunities can I explore today?*

That mental freedom is priceless. It's the space where creativity, ideas, and bold moves live. That's why the key isn't just increasing your income—it's holding the line on your lifestyle long enough to build real momentum. Because the middle is where people stall out. But if you stay disciplined, you can blast past it and into freedom.

THE POWER OF FOCUSED DEBT PAYOFF

I know crushing debt all too well. When my wife and I moved to Florida during the pandemic, we were already carrying more than $100,000 in debt. Eventually, with back taxes added in, that number climbed to nearly $200,000. I can't describe how heavy that felt. It wasn't just the big number staring at me on a statement—it was the monthly payments that came with it.

When I was driving DoorDash, I remember running the math: Between car payments, credit cards, and IRS debt, we owed about $2,100 a month just to cover the minimums. I'd put in a long week of deliveries, come home with $500, and feel completely defeated knowing that every penny would be swallowed by debt payments. None of it could go to food, savings, or investing—it was like working just to stay broke.

We hit a breaking point. We realized delivering food or even my wife's new job wasn't going to save us fast enough. So we got laser focused and built a two-year plan. We already had our real estate licenses, so we decided that every penny we made from closings would go straight to bills and debt. When TikTok started paying creators, I took 90 percent of that income—even on big months (15K–20K)—and dumped it directly onto the debt. At one point, we were each working multiple jobs, but slowly, piece by piece, we started whittling it down.

And here's what happened: As the balances shrank, our freedom grew. My wife was eventually able to quit one of her jobs. I stopped delivering food. The $2,100 in monthly minimums dropped to $600, and that alone felt like a massive raise. When we saw our debt fall from $197,000 down to $35,000, we could finally see the light at the end of the tunnel.

That's when it hit me: Debt isn't just numbers on a page. It's a financial prison that steals your time, your energy, and your future. But with a focused plan, you can break free—and fast.

Now I'm hoping if you are reading this, you aren't as weighed down with debt as we were, which could make this journey a bit simpler for you.

Let's say you're $20,000 in debt and decide to pick up a second job that earns you $2,000 a month waiting tables on nights and weekends. Yes, it will be grueling. Yes, it will mean late nights and giving up some of your free time. But in just ten months, that debt is gone—completely wiped out. That's not just a financial reset; it's a life reset.

Here's the trap most people fall into: The moment they earn extra money, they immediately upgrade their lifestyle. A vacation. A new laptop. Nights out. At first, it feels amazing—like a reward for all the hard work. But then five years go by, and they're still in debt, still stuck in the same grind, because that extra income never went toward freedom.

The truth is simple: *If you want to escape debt, you need intensity and focus.* Every extra dollar has to go to war on what you owe. Think of each dollar as a little soldier. You can either send it out to die on credit card interest—or you can send it to fight for your freedom.

Let's put this into perspective. A $20,000 balance at 20 percent interest could mean a $400 monthly payment. To make that $400, you actually have to earn $500 before taxes. That's $6,000 a year—gone. All just to tread water. Now imagine wiping out that debt. You've just given yourself an instant $400 raise, every month, for the rest of your life. That's a permanent reward for a temporary sacrifice.

THREE PROVEN WAYS TO PAY OFF DEBT

There isn't a one-size-fits-all solution to crushing debt. The right strategy depends on your personality, income, and tolerance for delayed gratification. Here are three proven approaches—with real examples—so you can decide which path works best for you.

1. THE SNOWBALL METHOD (MOMENTUM)

This approach focuses on building *psychological wins* first. You pay off your smallest debt while making minimum payments on the others. Once that first debt is gone, you roll its payment into the next one, and so on.

Example:

- Credit card #1: $1,000 balance at 18 percent interest ($50 minimum)
- Credit card #2: $5,000 balance at 22 percent interest ($150 minimum)
- Student loan: $15,000 balance at 6 percent interest ($200 minimum)

Let's say you can throw an extra $300 a month toward debt. With the snowball method, you'd pay $350 toward the $1,000 card ($50 minimum + $300 extra). That card would be gone in three months. Now you've freed up $50 in payments.

Next, you'd roll that $350 into card number two, making your new payment $500 a month ($150 minimum + $350 snowball). That card would be gone in about ten months.

Now you roll the $500 into your student loan, paying $700 a month ($200 minimum + $500 snowball). That loan would be gone in a little over two years.

Why it works: You get *fast wins* that build momentum and confidence. You feel progress early, which keeps you motivated.

2. THE AVALANCHE METHOD (MATH)

This approach focuses on saving the most money in the long term. You attack the highest-interest debt first while making minimum payments on the rest.

Example (same debts as above):

- Credit card #1: $1,000 at 18 percent ($50 minimum)
- Credit card #2: $5,000 at 22 percent ($150 minimum)
- Student loan: $15,000 at 6 percent ($200 minimum)

Here, you'd pay minimums on the $1,000 card and the student loan, then throw your extra $300 at credit card number two (the highest interest with 22 percent).

So you'd be paying $450 a month (that's $150 minimum + $300 extra) toward card #2. That debt would be gone in about twelve months. Then you'd roll that full $450 into card #1, wiping it out in just two months. Now with card #1's $50 minimum gone plus your $450, you'd have $500 a month to throw at the student loan, clearing it in about two and a half years.

Why it works: Mathematically, you'll pay *less interest overall* than with the snowball method. The downside? It takes longer to get that first "win," which can feel discouraging for some people.

3. DEBT CONSOLIDATION (SIMPLIFY AND LOWER INTEREST)

If you feel buried under multiple payments, consolidation can help. The goal is to roll your debts into a single payment—ideally at a lower interest rate—so more of your money goes toward principal, not interest.

Example:

- Credit card #1: $6,000 at 22 percent interest ($180 minimum)
- Credit card #2: $4,000 at 20 percent interest ($120 minimum)
- Personal loan: $10,000 at 12 percent interest ($250 minimum)

That's:

- Total debt = $20,000
- Total monthly minimums = $550

Now imagine you consolidate all $20,000 into a personal loan at 9 percent interest with a fixed $415 monthly payment.

That saves you:

- $135 per month extra that you can put toward principal and ideally even more on top of that.
- Thousands in interest if you stick to the new schedule.

Or, if you qualify for a zero percent balance transfer card with a 12–18-month intro period, you could transfer your $10,000 in credit card debt and aggressively pay it off interest free during that window.

The caution: Consolidation only works if you change your habits. If you consolidate and then start swiping your cards again, you're just stacking new debt on top of old. Used wisely, though, it's a powerful reset button.

THE CAR TRAP

Let's talk about one of the biggest financial traps in America: cars.

We love them. They're status symbols, comfort machines, even extensions of our identity. But the way most of us finance them? Financial quicksand.

Here's the harsh reality:

A brand-new $40,000 car loses nearly half its value in five years. By the time you've finished your loan, that shiny new ride is worth around $18,000. That's a $22,000 loss—before you even count the 5–8 percent interest you've been paying along the way. Add that in, and the "real" cost of your $40,000 car might be closer to $45,000–$50,000.

Now, let's compare two people:

Person A

- Buys a new $40,000 car.
- Payment = ~$700/month for sixty months.
- After five years, trades it in for maybe $18,000 and immediately rolls into another loan.

- Net result? They've spent tens of thousands to "rent" a depreciating asset, and the cycle never ends.
- Over decades, this habit can add up to *hundreds of thousands of dollars lost*, money that could have been building wealth in real estate or the stock market.

Person B

- Buys a reliable used car for $12,000.
- Pays it off in two years, then drives it for another seven.
- After year two, instead of sending $700/month to the bank, they invest it in the stock market.
- Just five years of $700 invested in the stock market at an 8 percent annual return (with dividends reinvested) could grow to *nearly $400,000 over 30 years*—even if they never invest another dime.
- The difference? Both drove cars, but one drove themself into perpetual debt while the other drove toward financial freedom.

Person B can still reward themself later. Once their investments are working for them and their retirement is on track, they could buy or lease the car of their dreams—this time from a place of strength, not desperation.

Because at the end of the day, a car is just a tool. The real question: Is your car driving you closer to freedom—or keeping you stuck in another financial cycle?

Note, this isn't just about cars. The same principle applies to housing, lifestyle, and almost every money decision: If you can afford $600/month on a car, buy one for $400 and invest the other $200. If you can afford $1,700 in rent, get a $1,500 place and invest the difference.

Those small shifts don't feel like sacrifices in the moment, but over time they add up to life-changing wealth.

And that's the perfect transition into the next idea: Getting ahead today isn't only about cutting expenses or saving diligently—it's about finding ways to accelerate your path to financial freedom so you don't have to wait until sixty-five to start living life on your own terms.

BUILDING TOWARD FINANCIAL FREEDOM

For many people, sticking to a steady, predictable job and consistently investing over time will lead to a solid retirement. It's not flashy, but it works—especially if you stay disciplined.

But not everyone wants to follow that traditional path. Some feel called to venture into self-employment or entrepreneurship. That route can be riskier—especially if you're not balancing it with consistent investing—but if you pull it off, it can lead to freedom or early retirement.

The key is not to think only in terms of saving but also in terms of ownership—of assets, businesses, or skills. That's where the real acceleration happens. Instead of asking "How can I slowly build toward retirement at sixty-five or seventy?" ask: "What steps can I take now to create financial stability and flexibility decades earlier?"

While you're letting your investments grow, also explore opportunities like:

- **Real estate:** House hacking, rentals, or commercial properties
- **Crypto and blockchain:** High risk, high reward if done wisely
- **Sales and high-ticket closing:** The most powerful skill you can learn
- **Building a business:** From e-commerce to local services
- **Content creation:** Podcasting, YouTube, TikTok—monetizing your expertise

- **Tech and AI:** Staying ahead of the industries shaping the future

The bottom line: The biggest wealth-building opportunities come from owning something, not just saving. The earlier you lean into that, the sooner you'll build not just wealth but freedom.

And most of us don't start with ownership—we start with a paycheck. Using that paycheck for stability while you build can be one of the strongest stepping stones toward financial freedom.

REFRAME YOUR NINE-TO-FIVE: FROM GRIND TO STABILITY TOOL

If you're one of the lucky ones who genuinely enjoys your nine-to-five, maximize it. Take advantage of the tools it gives you—a 401(k) match, affordable health insurance, steady income—and use that stability to build your freedom. Don't think of retirement accounts as something you'll only touch in thirty years. As you become debt free and start investing heavily in the market or real estate, that growing nest egg gives you options. Ten years from now, if your industry shifts or you want to pivot, you'll have a cushion. That kind of security doesn't just buy freedom later—it allows you to breathe easier during the climb.

For those who feel stuck in the grind and dream of eventually leaving the nine-to-five, here's a healthier way to see it: Your job isn't a prison. It's a stability tool.

Your paycheck covers the essentials—the rent, the groceries, the insurance. That safety net means you don't have to drain every dollar from your side hustle just to survive. Instead, you can reinvest those dollars into skills, assets, or a business that builds long-term wealth. Think of your nine-to-five like training wheels: You don't rip them off after your first wobbly ride. You keep them on until your balance is strong enough that taking them off won't send you crashing.

Take James and Sarah. James dreamed of leaving his nine-to-five to pursue content creation, but he wasn't willing to risk his family's stability. Meanwhile, Sarah's corporate job provided health insurance, a 401(k) match, and a reliable paycheck. That foundation allowed James to reinvest every dollar from his side hustle back into the business. Eventually, they used that money to buy investment properties, which today generate $10,000 a month in passive income. They didn't abandon their jobs too soon—they leveraged them until the side hustle became a true wealth engine.

This is also what my wife and I have been doing. With her stable nine-to-five, we had excellent health insurance, a 401(k) with company match, and her income alone covered all our bills. That freed me to focus entirely on growing our business and tackling our debt. Every dollar from content, affiliates, podcasting, and real estate went toward paying down what we owed, instead of just keeping the lights on. If she had quit too soon, that money would have been consumed by bills instead of building our future. It's harder if you're on your own, but not impossible—the key is timing. You want to make sure your business is ready to carry the weight before you let go of your safety net.

Now let's look at Mike. He was making $4,000 a month selling custom sneakers online, on top of his day job. After one good month, he quit his nine-to-five. Overnight, every dollar from his business had to cover rent, food, and insurance. He cut marketing, downgraded materials, and lost momentum. Within a year, he was broke, burned out, and back at a job—this time with a struggling business on his hands.

The lesson? Don't throw away stability before you've built sustainability. Too many people quit their jobs too soon and choke their side hustle before it has a chance to breathe. But if you hold on to your nine-to-five long enough, you give yourself room to grow. That first big commission check doesn't have to cover rent—it can buy a rental property. That first viral paycheck doesn't have to pay bills—it can be reinvested in better equipment, ads, or mentorship.

Your nine-to-five can be a wonderful bridge. Use it wisely, and it can fund your escape from the rat race. And once you cross that bridge, you'll be standing on solid ground—ready to move into the final stage of the new American Dream: building assets that work for you, instead of you always working for them.

FROM SURVIVING TO THRIVING

Right now, many of you may be in a tough position—and it's likely not your fault. We followed the default path, the one that built the boomer generation into the wealthiest in history. But policies shifted, costs exploded, and wages lagged behind. That same path doesn't work the way it once did.

So here's the question: *What did the last three years of your life look like?*

If you're buried in debt, stuck in a job you hate, or living in a place that drains you, what choices will you make to ensure the next three years don't look the same? The last thing you want is to be in the exact same spot—or worse—just a few years down the road.

Turning things around isn't easy. Paying off debt, growing a career, or starting a business requires discipline and sacrifice. And while it's unfair that the system stacked the odds against you, the truth is, no one's coming to fix it for you. But we can be the change.

I know a lot of what we've covered can feel heavy. You'd think that in a country this wealthy, filled with so much talent and innovation, the road to success for hardworking Americans would be easier by now. With the technology we have today, we should be working four-day workweeks, earning more, and enjoying more freedom. That's not entitlement—that's just math. The generations before us put in the grueling work to get us here, but somewhere along the way, policy after policy chipped away at the ladder, making it harder for our generation to climb.

But here's the truth: *Hope isn't lost.* In fact, it's just beginning.

Our generation is the most resourceful, educated, and connected generation of all time. There are 140 million millennials and Gen Zers in the US alone—and millions more across every generation who want to see change. What a story arc it would be if history remembered us as the generation that was pushed down, divided, and dismissed—but refused to stay there. Instead, we banded together, shared our stories, fought for a fairer system, and rebuilt the American Dream on new terms.

That's the fight worth showing up for. Yes, corporations and lobbyists have spent trillions to keep us divided and distracted. Yes, the system is designed to resist change. But here's what they can't take from us: our ability to take control of our own finances, our families, and our communities—right now.

That means:

- Paying down debt so we're no longer chained to the past;
- Refusing the car and credit traps that keep us stuck;
- Prioritizing investing as highly as food, shelter, healthcare, and education;
- Teaching our children early what most of us were never taught.

Because once we build that foundation, something incredible happens: freedom. Freedom to take risks, to pivot when the world changes, to explore new opportunities, and to actually live the lives we've imagined.

And that's what makes our generation unique. We don't have the luxury of following one predictable path for forty years. The world is changing too fast for that. Instead, we get to write a new version of the American Dream—one built on adaptability, ownership, and community.

The old dream was about stability. The new dream is about freedom.

So let's stop surviving. Let's start thriving. Let's build a future where our work moves our lives forward, our money works for us instead of against us, and our time is spent with the people who matter most. That's the new American Dream. And it's ours to claim.

ACKNOWLEDGMENTS

First and foremost, I want to thank Val Frankel, my agent, for believing in this project from its earliest days. You saw my work, recognized its potential, and helped me take my voice and turn it into a book. From shaping the proposal to connecting me with BenBella, my publisher, your support made this entire journey possible. I'm deeply grateful for your guidance, your belief, and your passion for this project.

I also want to thank Claire Schulz, my editor at BenBella Books. Through every stage of this process, your steady presence and thoughtful edits helped turn this manuscript into a finished book. You brought such care, thoughtfulness, and integrity to every part of this book, and it shows on every page.

Greg Newton Brown, my developmental editor, thank you for your early editorial notes and big-picture insight, which reshaped this book in ways that still echo through every chapter. Your thoughtful notes and conversations helped me see what this book really wanted to be, and I'm deeply grateful for the way you helped me get there.

Scott Calamar, copyeditor, thank you for bringing a sharp, thoughtful, and often wonderfully witty perspective to the later draft of this book. Your feedback, questions, and insights helped strengthen the ideas and made the final version stronger, clearer, and more grounded. I'm grateful for the care you brought to those final passes.

To the entire team at BenBella Books—thank you for betting on me, for elevating this project, and for making the publishing process supportive, thoughtful and incredibly enjoyable. From shaping the manuscript to designing, producing, and bringing it into the world, your care and expertise meant the world to me.

To Glenn Yeffeth, CEO of BenBella Books, thank you for your belief in this book from the very beginning. From our very first conversation, your warmth and enthusiasm made this book feel right at home. And to Adrienne Lang, Publisher, thank you for believing in me and this project and for helping guide how it was positioned and brought into the world.

I'm also grateful to the marketing and sales team who are helping this book find its readers: Jennifer Canzoneri, Chief Marketing Officer, for leading the overall vision; Kellie Doherty, Senior Marketing Associate, for the hands-on work of launching this book and helping me share this message with the world; and Susan Welte, Sales Manager, for everything you've done to get this book into stores and into people's hands.

Thank you to Sarah Avinger, Art Director, and Morgan Carr, Cover Designer, for bringing this book's visual identity—and its cover—to life; Monica Lowry, Production Director, Jessika Rieck, Production Director, Aaron Edmiston, Interior Designer, and Kim Broderick, Production Editor, for keeping everything running smoothly behind the scenes; Rachel Phares, Rights Manager, for expanding this book's reach; Alicia Kania, Vendor Content Manager, for making sure it shows up everywhere it should; and Madeline Grigg, Publishing Associate, for all the support that helped keep this project moving forward.

To my incredible social media audience: this book exists because of you. Your comments, questions, and stories challenged me, inspired me, and shaped what these pages became. Thank you for trusting me with your experiences and for being part of this journey. And to fellow creators who do meaningful, educational work—you push me to keep raising my own bar.

And to my wife, Alyssa—thank you for being there through every version of this book, for patiently listening to far more about quantitative easing, Super PACs, and private equity than any one person should have to. You watched this idea grow from scattered notes on my desk and countless short-form videos into something real, and you never stopped encouraging me along the way. Your love, patience, and steady belief in me carried me every step of the way. I could not have written this book without you.

To my friends and family, thank you for always meeting my new ideas and new adventures with excitement and support. Having your unconditional love gives me the confidence to take risks and chase big ideas. Mom and Dad, thank you for celebrating the wins with me and for listening when I need to vent or feel discouraged. Your love and support mean the world to me.

Finally, thank you to you, the reader. Picking up a book is a choice. Thank you for choosing this one. I hope it gives you clarity, courage, and the tools to see the system differently—and to act.

NOTES

1 National Association of Realtors, "Existing-Home Sales Retreated 3.3% in June; Monthly Median Sales Price Reached Second-Highest Amount Ever," GlobeNewswire, July 20, 2023, https://www.globenewswire.com/news-release/2023/07/20/2708362/0/en/Existing-Home-Sales-Retreated-3-3-in-June-Monthly-Median-Sales-Price-Reached-Second-Highest-Amount-Ever.html.

2 Gloria Guzman and Melissa Kollar, "Income in the United States: 2023," United States Census Bureau, September 10, 2024, https://www.census.gov/library/publications/2024/demo/p60-282.html.

3 Emmie Martin, "Here's How Much Housing Costs Have Skyrocketed over the Last 50 Years," CNBC, June 23, 2017, https://www.cnbc.com/2017/06/23/how-much-housing-prices-have-risen-since-1940.html, citing National Association of Realtors historical home-price data.

4 US Census Bureau, "Nearly Half of Renter Households Are Cost-Burdened," September 12, 2024, https://www.census.gov/newsroom/press-releases/2024/renter-households-cost-burdened-race.html.

5 "Americans now hold over $1.7 trillion in outstanding student loan debt, reflecting a dramatic increase over recent decades." Source: AAUW, "Where We Stand: Student Debt," January 2022, https://www.aauw.org/resources/policy/position-student-debt/.

6 Alice Gibbs, "Map Reveals States with the Most Expensive Childcare," *Newsweek*, November 8, 2025, https://www.newsweek.com/map-reveals-states-expensive-childcare-11009727.

7 US Bureau of Labor Statistics, "Consumer Price Index for All Urban Consumers: Food at Home in US City Average [CUSR0000SAF11]," retrieved from FRED, Federal Reserve Bank of St. Louis, January 16, 2026, https://fred.stlouisfed.org/series/CUSR0000SAF11; "Consumer Price Index for All Urban Consumers: Rent of Primary Residence in US City Average [CUSR0000SEHA]," retrieved from FRED, Federal Reserve Bank of St. Louis, January 16, 2026, https://fred.

stlouisfed.org/series/CUSR0000SEHA; "Consumer Price Index for All Urban Consumers: Gasoline (All Types) in US City Average [CUUR0000SETB01]," retrieved from FRED, Federal Reserve Bank of St. Louis, January 16, 2026, https://fred.stlouisfed.org/series/CUUR0000SETB01.

8 National Association of Realtors, "Highlights from the Profile of Home Buyers and Sellers," 2025, https://www.nar.realtor/research-and-statistics/researchl-reports/highlights-from-the-profile-of-home-buyers-and-sellers.

9 Ana Tereza Solá, "Average age of first-time homebuyers is 38, an all-time high. Here's what that says about the real estate market," CNBC, November 5, 2024, https://www.cnbc.com/2024/11/05/the-average-age-of-first-time-us-homebuyers-is-38-an-all-time-high.html.

10 Robert Davis, "Millennials Are Now the 'Roommate Generation' After Being Squeezed Out of Homeownership by High Housing Costs, Said Redfin CEO," *Business Insider*, January 9, 2023, https://www.businessinsider.com/millennials-are-now-the-roommate-generation-redfin-ceo-says-2023-1.

11 Historical price data (from the US Bureau of Labor Statistics Consumer Price Index) show that consumer television sets in the mid-1980s still sold for **several hundred dollars**, with average price levels around **$700–$750** for a typical set in **1985–1987** before later price declines. Ian Webster, "Televisions price inflation since 1960," Official Data Inflation Calculator, January 9, 2026, https://www.in2013dollars.com/Televisions/price-inflation/1960.

12 CD prices declined into the mid-1980s. Bondsy, "The Compact Disc Is Now 40 Years Old," Woodward Community Media, August 17, 2022, https://wcmspi.com/2022/08/17/the-compact-disc-is-now-40-years-old/.

13 Consumer microwave ovens (e.g., Litton models) were priced at approximately **$289–$329** in 1985. Morris County Library, "Historic Prices: 1980s–1985," accessed January 9, 2026, https://www.mclib.info/Research/Morris-County-Library-Reference-Guides/Historic-Prices/Historic-Prices-1980s/Historic-Prices-1985.

14 Motorola DynaTAC 8000X (first consumer handheld mobile phone, 1984) sold for approximately **$4,000** at launch. National Museum of American History, Smithsonian Institution, "Dynatac Cellular Telephone," accessed January 9, 2026, https://americanhistory.si.edu/collections/object/nmah_1191361.

15 The suggested retail price of the Macintosh Advanced personal computer was **$2,495**. Regis McKenna Public Relations, "Apple Introduces Macintosh Advanced Personal Computer," January 24, 1984, via Alex Soojung Kim-Pang and Wendy Marinaccio, "Making the Macintosh: Technology and Culture in Silicon Valley," June 6, 2000, https://web.stanford.edu/dept/SUL/sites/mac/primary/docs/pr1.html.

16 Ryan Knutson and Jessica Mendoza, cohosts, *The Journal*, podcast, "JP Morgan CEO Jamie Dimon on What's Next for the Economy," produced by *The Wall Street Journal*, April 26, 2024, https://www.wsj.com/podcasts/the-journal/jp

-morgan-ceo-jamie-dimon-on-what-next-for-the-economy/88c92388-fbb0-4194-bc05-13cceea3e64b.

17 About **67 percent of Americans** say they live paycheck to paycheck. Karen Webster, "Who Is the Paycheck-to-Paycheck Consumer in America?" PYMNTS, March 11, 2025, https://www.pymnts.com/consumer-finance/2025/who-is-the-paycheck-to-paycheck-consumer-in-america/.

18 The estimated personal savings rate (percentage of disposable personal income saved) in 2025 was near 4 percent. US Department of Commerce, Bureau of Economic Analysis, "Personal Saving Rate," accessed January 9, 2026, https://www.bea.gov/data/income-saving/personal-saving-rate.

19 Corporate profits have been elevated in recent years: e.g., 7.6 percent growth in 2023 and 5.1 percent in 2024. US Department of Commerce, Bureau of Economic Analysis, "Corporate Profits," accessed January 9, 2026, https://www.bea.gov/data/income-saving/corporate-profits.

20 Francis Torres, "U.S. Opinions on Housing Affordability: A BPC/NHC/Morning Consult Poll," Bipartisan Policy Center, June 10, 2024, https://bipartisanpolicy.org/article/opinions-on-housing-affordability-poll/.

21 U.S. Bureau of Labor Statistics, "Consumer Unit Characteristics: Percent Homeowner by Age: from Age 25 to 34 [CXUHOMEOWNLB0403M]," retrieved from FRED, Federal Reserve Bank of St. Louis, January 9, 2026, https://fred.stlouisfed.org/series/CXUHOMEOWNLB0403M.

22 Medical debt—personal debt incurred from unpaid medical bills—is a leading cause of bankruptcy in the US and affects nearly a third of working-age adults. Maanasa Kona and Vrudhi Raimugia, "State Protections Against Medical Debt: A Look at Policies Across the U.S.," Commonwealth Fund, July 16, 2025, https://www.commonwealthfund.org/publications/fund-reports/2025/jul/state-protections-against-medical-debt-look-policies-across-us.

23 The US fertility rate was 1.599 children per woman in 2024. Mike Stobbe, "The US Fertility Rate Reached a New Low in 2024, CDC Data Shows," AP News, July 24, 2025, https://apnews.com/article/532c4f43f420f29b32212db9cfa0e0af.

24 Average tuition and fees at public four-year colleges increased from about $4,900 to nearly $11,000 (in inflation-adjusted dollars). Jamie Merisotis, "The Real Cost of Education—For Students, Families, and the Nation," *Footnotes*, a Magazine of the American Sociological Association 51, no. 2 (Spring 2023), https://www.asanet.org/footnotes-article/the-real-cost-of-education-for-students-families-and-the-nation/.

25 The highest funded states spend more than twice as much per student as the lowest funded states. Danielle Farrie and Robert Kim, "Making the Grade 2024: Education Funding Disparities Persist," Education Law Center, 2024, https://edlawcenter.org/research/making-the-grade-2024/.

26 Centers for Disease Control and Prevention, "Youth Risk Behavior Survey Data Summary & Trends Report: 2013–2023," *Morbidity and Mortality Weekly*

Report 73, suppl. 4, October 10, 2024, https://www.cdc.gov/mmwr/volumes/73/su/pdfs/su7304a9-H.pdf.

27 Pew Research Center, "Public Trust in Government: 1958–2023," December 4, 2025, https://www.pewresearch.org/politics/2023/09/19/public-trust-in-government-1958-2023/.

28 Matt Phillips, "The Rich Now Own a Record Share of Stocks," Axios, January 10, 2024, https://www.axios.com/2024/01/10/wealthy-own-record-share-stock-market.

29 Economic Policy Institute, "The Productivity–Pay Gap: Where Are We Now?" updated September 3, 2025, https://www.epi.org/productivity-pay-gap/.

30 Bryan Robinson, "Latest Four-Day Workweek Study Shows Mental Health Benefits—but Will It Catch On Where You Work?" *Forbes*, July 30, 2025, https://www.forbes.com/sites/bryanrobinson/2025/07/30/latest-4-day-workweek-study-shows-mental-health-benefits-but-will-it-catch-on-where-you-work/.

31 Robert R. Callis, "Younger Householders Drove Rebound in US Homeownership," United States Census Bureau, July 25, 2023, https://www.census.gov/library/stories/2023/07/younger-householders-drove-rebound-in-homeownership.html.

32 Treh Manhertz, "US Housing Market Value Hits $55.1 Trillion," Zillow, September 8, 2025, https://www.zillow.com/research/housing-market-value-1-trillion-35518/.

33 Alexis Wray, "Housing Affordability Crisis: Many Americans Are Spending 50% of Their Income on Housing, New Study Finds," Reckon, July 2024, https://www.reckon.news/justice/2024/07/housing-affordability-crisis-many-americans-are-spending-50-of-their-income-on-housing-new-study-finds.html.

34 In 2010, the median sales price of existing homes sold in the United States was approximately $173,000. U.S. Department of Housing and Urban Development, "2010 Overview of U.S. Housing Market Conditions," March 10, 2011, https://www.huduser.gov/portal/elist/2011-Mar10.html.

35 International comparisons consistently show that countries such as Sweden, Norway, and Denmark rank higher than the United States on measures of happiness, health, and work-life balance; that Canada and Germany provide universal healthcare and low-cost or tuition-free public higher education; and that Australia has shorter average working hours and higher average wages, despite having a smaller gross domestic product than the United States. See John F. Helliwell, Richard Layard, Jeffrey D. Sachs, Jan-Emmanuel De Neve, Lara B. Aknin, and Shun Wang, eds., *World Happiness Report 2025*, University of Oxford: Wellbeing Research Centre, 2025, https://worldhappiness.report/; OECD, "Education," "Employment," and "Health" databases, accessed January 9, 2026, https://www.oecd.org/education/, https://www.oecd.org/employment/, and https://www.oecd.org/health/.

36 US Census Bureau, "Median Gross Rents: Unadjusted," accessed January 9,

2026, https://www2.census.gov/programs-surveys/decennial/tables/time-series/coh-grossrents/grossrents-unadj.txt.

37 US Census Bureau, "Table K202511: Median Gross Rent (Dollars)," accessed January 9, 2026, https://data.census.gov/table/ACSSE2024.K202511.

38 "California Rental Market Trends," RentCafe, December 18, 2025, https://www.rentcafe.com/average-rent-market-trends/us/ca/.

39 ZipRecruiter, "Entry Level College Grads Salary," accessed January 9, 2026, https://www.ziprecruiter.com/Salaries/Entry-Level-College-Grads-Salary.

40 Economic Policy Institute, "The Productivity–Pay Gap: Where Are We Now?" updated September 3, 2025, https://www.epi.org/productivity-pay-gap/.

41 Josh Bivens and Jori Kandra, "CEO Pay Has Skyrocketed 1,209% Since 1978," Economic Policy Institute, September 21, 2023, https://www.epi.org/publication/ceo-pay-in-2022/.

42 US Bureau of Labor Statistics, "Consumer Price Index for All Urban Consumers (CPIAUCSL)," available via Federal Reserve Economic Data (FRED), January 16, 2026, https://fred.stlouisfed.org/series/CPIAUCSL.

43 US Bureau of Economic Analysis, "Corporate Profits," accessed January 9, 2026, https://www.bea.gov/data/income-saving/corporate-profits; US Bureau of Labor Statistics, "Real Earnings Summary," December 18, 2025, https://www.bls.gov/news.release/realer.nr0.htm.

44 Corporate after-tax profits rose from approximately **$2.21 trillion in 2020** to about **$3.50 trillion in 2024,** an increase of nearly **60 percent** (US Bureau of Economic Analysis, "Corporate Profits: Profits After Tax (A055RC1A027NBEA"), retrieved from Federal Reserve Economic Data (FRED), January 16, 2026, https://fred.stlouisfed.org/series/A055RC1A027NBEA). US billionaire wealth rose from about $2.95 trillion in March 2020 to $5.53 trillion in March 2024, an increase of ~80 percent (Chuck Collins and Omar Ocampo, "Total US Billionaire Wealth: Up 88 Percent over Four Years," Inequality.org, March 18, 2024, https://inequality.org/article/billionaire-wealth-up-88-percent-over-four-years/). The richest 1 percent of US households controlled roughly $33 trillion in net worth in 2020 and about $49 trillion in 2024 (about a 30.4 percent and 30.8 percent share of total US household wealth, in those respective years), implying about $16 trillion in net-worth growth over that period (Govind Bhutada, "Visualized: The 1%'s Share of U.S. Wealth Over Time (1989–2024)," Visual Capitalist, February 8, 2025, https://www.visualcapitalist.com/visualized-the-1s-share-of-u-s-wealth-over-time-1989-2024/).

45 Jessica Nix, "U.S. Births Last Year Fell to Lowest Since 1979," *Time*, April 25, 2024, https://time.com/6970873/us-declining-birth-rate-2023-total/.

46 University of California Office of Federal Governmental Relations, "Why It's Time to Double the Pell," March 2022, https://www.ucop.edu/federal-governmental-relations/_files/fact-sheets/uc-dtp-factsheet.pdf.

47 Lance Dinino, "How Administrative Bloat Is Killing American Higher Education," *The Bowdoin Review*, February 7, 2024, https://students.bowdoin

.edu/bowdoin-review/features/death-by-a-thousand-emails-how-administrative-bloat-is-killing-american-higher-education/.

48 Beth Akers, "Consumption Amenities in Higher Education," *Brookings Institution*, February 6, 2013, https://www.brookings.edu/research/consumption-amenities-in-higher-education/; Jon Marcus, "From Google ads to NFL sponsorships: Colleges throw billions at marketing themselves to attract students," The Hechinger Report, October 1, 2021, https://hechingerreport.org/with-competition-up-enrollment-down-colleges-are-spending-billions-on-marketing-and-advertising/.

49 National Center for Education Statistics, "Table 330.10: [CORRECTED] Average undergraduate tuition, fees, room, and board rates charged for full-time students in degree-granting postsecondary institutions, by level and control of institution: Selected academic years, 1963-64 through 2021-22," in *Digest of Education Statistics: 2022*, accessed December 23, 2025, https://nces.ed.gov/programs/digest/d22/tables/dt22_330.10.asp.

50 Jennifer Ma, Matea Pender, and Meghan Oster, *Trends in College Pricing and Student Aid 2024* (College Board, 2024), https://research.collegeboard.org/media/pdf/Trends-in-College-Pricing-and-Student-Aid-2024-ADA.pdf.

51 Melanie Hanson, "Average Student Loan Payment," Education Data Initiative, March 11, 2025, https://educationdata.org/average-student-loan-payment.

52 Barack Obama, "Remarks by the President on College Affordability," May 31, 2013, https://obamawhitehouse.archives.gov/the-press-office/2013/05/31/remarks-president-college-affordability.

53 Consumer Financial Protection Bureau, "CFPB Takes Action to Address Illegal Debt Collection Practices by the National Collegiate Student Loan Trusts," January 16, 2025, https://www.consumerfinance.gov/about-us/newsroom/.cfpb-takes-action-to-address-illegal-debt-collection-practices-by-the-national-collegiate-student-loan-trusts/; Freddie Smith, host, "Is College Debt the Next 2008 Crisis? *The Freddie Smith Podcast* with Hannah Maruyama | Episode 001," YouTube video, published April 3, 2025, https://www.youtube.com/watch?v=bDTZeFQezUI.

54 Anthony P. Carnevale, Stephen J. Rose, and Ban Cheah, *The College Payoff: Education, Occupations, Lifetime Earnings* (Georgetown University Center on Education and the Workforce, 2011), https://cew.georgetown.edu/cew-reports/the-college-payoff/.

55 Average tuition and fees at four-year public institutions were $804 in 1980–81 (National Center for Education Statistics, "Table 330.10. Average undergraduate tuition, fees, room, and board rates charged for full-time students in degree-granting postsecondary institutions, by level and control of institution: Selected academic years, 1963-64 through 2022-23," *Digest of Education Statistics*, December 2023, https://nces.ed.gov/programs/digest/d23/tables/dt23_330.10.asp); in comparison, average published in-state tuition and fees were approximately $12,000 at public four-year institutions in recent years (nominal

dollars) (College Board, "Trends in College Pricing: Highlights," accessed January 9, 2026, https://research.collegeboard.org/trends/college-pricing/highlights).

56 Heather Hannerich, "The Jobs and Degrees Underemployed College Graduates Have," Federal Reserve Bank of St. Louis, August 13, 2025, https://www.stlouisfed.org/open-vault/2025/aug/jobs-degrees-underemployed-college-graduates-have.

57 Venessa Wong, "A TikTok Hack Claims to Help Kids Retire with $4 Million—if Their Parents Can Stomach Some Major Sacrifices," MarketWatch, July 17, 2025, https://www.marketwatch.com/story/a-tiktok-hack-claims-to-help-kids-retire-with-4-million-if-their-parents-can-stomach-some-major-sacrifices-6613c046.

58 Brendan Ballou, "Private Equity Is Gutting America—and Getting Away with It," *New York Times*, April 28, 2023, https://www.nytimes.com/2023/04/28/opinion/private-equity.html.

59 "BlackRock Q2 2025 Slides: AUM Hits $12.5T as Alternatives Business Surges," Investing.com, July 15, 2025, https://www.investing.com/news/company-news/blackrock-q2-2025-slides-aum-hits-125t-as-alternatives-business-surges-93CH-4135168.

60 Antoine Gara, "Blackstone's $9.6 Billion Bet on the U.S. Housing Recovery Files to Go Public," *Forbes*, January 6, 2017, https://www.forbes.com/sites/antoinegara/2017/01/06/blackstones-big-bet-on-the-u-s-housing-recovery-files-to-go-public/.

61 Samantha Sharf, "Single-Family Rental Leaders Invitation Homes, Starwood Waypoint Homes To Combine," *Forbes*, August 10, 2017, https://www.forbes.com/sites/samanthasharf/2017/08/10/single-family-rental-leaders-invitation-homes-starwood-waypoint-homes-to-combine/.

62 Pari Sastry and David Wessel, "The Hutchins Center Explains: Quantitative Easing," Brookings, March 20, 2025 (updated), https://www.brookings.edu/articles/the-hutchins-center-explains-quantitative-easing/.

63 David Carey, "Bain, KKR, Vornado Suffer Wipeout in Toys 'R' Us Bankruptcy," Bloomberg, September 19, 2017, https://www.bloomberg.com/news/articles/2017-09-19/bain-kkr-vornado-suffer-wipeout-in-toys-r-us-bankruptcy.

64 According to the Federal Reserve's 2022 Survey of Consumer Finances, the median (50th-percentile) net worth of US households was approximately $192,900, meaning half of households have a higher net worth and half have a lower net worth. Trevor Jennewine, "Here's the Income and Net Worth You Need to Reach the Top 50% of American Households," The Motley Fool, May 9, 2024, https://www.nasdaq.com/articles/heres-the-income-and-net-worth-you-need-to-reach-the-top-50-of-american-households.

65 Fidelity Investments, "How Do Your Retirement Savings Stack Up?" updated 2024, https://www.fidelity.com/learning-center/personal-finance/average-retirement-savings.

66 4 Day Week Global, "The 4 Day Week UK Results," official pilot report (2022), https://www.4dayweek.com/uk-pilot-results.
67 Marta Nocchi, "The Four-Day Workweek Movement: Lessons from Belgian and Icelandic Models," IRIS Global, September 4, 2025, https://www.irisglobal.com/blog/four-day-workweek-movement/.
68 Karen Gilchrist, "Microsoft Japan 4-Day Work Week Experiment Sees Productivity Jump 40%," CNBC, November 4, 2019, https://www.cnbc.com/2019/11/04/microsoft-japan-4-day-work-week-experiment-sees-productivity-jump-40percent.html.
69 U.S. Bureau of Labor Statistics, "Labor Productivity and Costs," accessed 2025, https://www.bls.gov/productivity/; Economic Policy Institute, "CEO Pay Jumped Nearly 6% in 2024; CEOs Made 281 Times as Much as the Typical Worker," September 25, 2025, https://www.epi.org/press/ceo-pay-jumped-nearly-6-in-2024-ceos-made-281-times-as-much-as-the-typical-worker/.
70 Justin Holt, "A reappraisal of Keynes's 'Economic possibilities for our grandchildren,'" U.S. Bureau of Labor Statistics, May 2024, https://www.bls.gov/opub/mlr/2024/beyond-bls/a-reappraisal-of-keyness-economic-possibilities-for-our-grandchildren.htm.
71 Robert Frank, "The Wealth of the Top 1% Reaches a Record $52 Trillion," CNBC, October 3, 2025, https://www.cnbc.com/2025/10/03/the-wealth-of-the-top-1percent-reaches-a-record-52-trillion.html.
72 Board of Governors of the Federal Reserve System (US), "Net Worth Held by the Bottom 50% (1st to 50th Wealth Percentiles) [WFRBLB50107]," retrieved from FRED, Federal Reserve Bank of St. Louis, January 9, 2026, https://fred.stlouisfed.org/series/WFRBLB50107.
73 Renu Zaretsky, "Could Harris's Proposed Tax Increases Cover the Cost of Her Plans?" Tax Policy Center, October 10, 2024, https://taxpolicycenter.org/taxvox/could-harris-tax-increases-pay-her-policy-proposals.
74 "S&P 500 Q4 2022 Buybacks Tick Up, As 2022 Sets a Record," S&P Dow Jones Indices press release, March 21, 2023, https://www.spglobal.com/spdji/en/documents/index-news-and-announcements/20230321-sp-500-buyback-q4-final-press-release.pdf.
75 Publix Super Markets, "Facts & Figures," accessed January 9, 2026, https://corporate.publix.com/about-publix/company-overview/facts-figures.
76 Aaron McDade, "Costco's Average Hourly Wage Is Over $30. Here's How That Stacks Up," Investopedia, September 27, 2024, https://www.investopedia.com/costco-average-hourly-wage-30-how-that-stacks-up-national-average-8719513.
77 OpenSecrets, "2024 Outside Spending, by Super PAC," accessed January 12, 2026, https://www.opensecrets.org/outside-spending/super_pacs.
78 According to federal lobbying disclosures compiled by Bloomberg Government and OpenSecrets, annual spending to influence the U.S. federal government on public policy and legislation has consistently topped **$4 billion**, with the total reaching a record-high level in recent years. Bloomberg Government reported

federal lobbying expenditures at about **$4.5 billion** in 2024 and OpenSecrets data indicate similar totals.

79 New York City Campaign Finance Board, "How It Works," accessed January 12, 2026, https://www.nyccfb.info/program/how-it-works.

80 City of Seattle, "Democracy Voucher Program," accessed January 12, 2026, https://www.seattle.gov/democracyvoucher.

81 Maine operates this model under the Maine Clean Election Act, and Arizona runs a similar Clean Elections program. Maine Commission on Governmental Ethics and Election Practices, "Maine Clean Election Act," accessed January 12, 2026, https://www.maine.gov/ethics/candidates/maine-clean-election-act; Arizona Citizens Clean Elections Commission, "How Clean Funding Works," accessed January 12, 2026, https://www.azcleanelections.gov/run-for-office/how-clean-funding-works.

82 S&P Dow Jones Indices, "S&P 500 Q4 2022 Buybacks Tick up, as 2022 Sets a Record; Proforma Buyback Tax Would Have Reduced Operating Earnings by 0.51% for 2022," March 21, 2023, https://www.spglobal.com/spdji/en/documents/index-news-and-announcements/20230321-sp-500-buyback-q4-final-press-release.pdf.

83 S&P Global, "S&P 500 Q4 2023 Buybacks Increase 18.0% Compared to Q3, Full Year 2023 Shows Decline of 13.8% from 2022 Levels, Earnings Per Share Impact Continues to Decline; Buybacks Tax Reduced Q4 Operating Earnings by 0.44% and 2023 by 0.40%," March 18, 2024, https://www.spglobal.com/spdji/en/corporate-news/article/sp-500-q4-2023-buybacks-increase-180-compared-to-q3/.

84 S&P Dow Jones Indices, "S&P 500 Q4 2024 Buybacks Increase 7.4% and 2024 Expenditure Sets New Record by Increasing 18.5%; Earnings Per Share Increases from Buybacks Decline for the Quarter, as Q1 2025's Impact is Expected to Increase," March 19, 2025, https://www.spglobal.com/spdji/en/documents/index-news-and-announcements/20250319-sp-500-buybacks.pdf.

85 The Cayman Islands has a relatively small resident population—estimated at about 74,500 people in 2024, according to World Bank data—while its corporate registry includes over 118,000 registered companies. World Bank, "Population, Total – Cayman Islands," accessed January 12, 2026, https://data.worldbank.org/indicator/SP.POP.TOTL?locations=KY; Preetha Pillai and Rita Leung, "Why the Cayman Islands?," Conyers Global Insights, January 2025, https://www.conyers.com/publications/view/why-the-cayman-islands.

86 Estimates of potential revenue from a federal wealth tax vary by design and assumptions, but analyses of Senator Elizabeth Warren's proposed wealth tax by economists Emmanuel Saez and Gabriel Zucman and other researchers suggest it could raise on the order of hundreds of billions of dollars annually. For example, Saez and Zucman have estimated that a 2 percent tax on wealth above $50 million (with a 3 percent surtax above $1 billion) could raise roughly $212 billion in a single year and about $2.75 trillion over a decade, depending

on implementation and compliance assumptions. Emmanuel Saez and Gabriel Zucman, letter to Elizabeth Warren, January 18, 2019, https://gabriel-zucman.eu/files/saez-zucman-wealthtax-warren.pdf; Huaqun Li and Karl Smith, "Analysis of Sen. Warren and Sen. Sanders' Wealth Tax Plans," Tax Foundation, January 28, 2020, https://www.taxfoundation.org/research/all/federal/wealth-tax/.

87 Economic researchers have noted the significant valuation and administrative challenges associated with taxing unrealized capital gains—especially on illiquid assets—while some analyses view wealth taxation as conceptually more feasible. Spencer Bastrani and Daniel Waldenström, "Taxing the Wealthy: The Choice Between Wealth and Capital Income Taxation," CEPR/VoxEU, March 5, 2024, https://cepr.org/voxeu/columns/taxing-wealthy-choice-between-wealth-and-capital-income-taxation.

88 US federal revenue and budget data—including total receipts, outlays, and deficits—are compiled and published by the US Department of the Treasury. For fiscal year 2025, total federal revenue was approximately $5.23 trillion, total spending was about $7.01 trillion, and the resulting deficit was roughly $1.78 trillion.

89 Peter G. Peterson Foundation, "How Does the Capital Gains Tax Work Now, and What Are Some Proposed Reforms?," updated August 26, 2024, https://www.pgpf.org/article/how-does-the-capital-gains-tax-work-now-and-what-are-some-proposed-reforms/; Tax Foundation, "Historical US Federal Capital Gains Tax Rates & Collections, 1913-2025," August 15, 2025, https://taxfoundation.org/data/all/federal/federal-capital-gains-tax-collections-historical-data/.

INDEX

D

I

J

K

W

ABOUT THE AUTHOR

Photo by Alyssa Tabit Smith

Freddie Smith is an Emmy Award–winning actor turned economic storyteller whose unexpected journey—from Hollywood soundstages to becoming one of the internet's most trusted voices on money and inequality—has resonated with millions. With over a billion views across TikTok, Instagram, and YouTube, Freddie breaks down the hidden forces shaping our financial lives and exposes the systems that have left millennials and Gen Z behind. His viral content has sparked national conversations about housing, wages, debt, and the future of the American Dream. Freddie lives with his wife in Florida, where he continues to create content, write, and advocate for economic clarity and generational change.